FEAR NOT THE FALL

To Dr. Carls,

Powerful woman,

Billie Gregory

Thanks!

ALSO BY BILLIE JEAN YOUNG

The Child of Too (1982)

Fannie Lou Hamer: This Little Light . . . (1983)

THE CONECUH SERIES
CELEBRATING DIVERSITY IN THE SOUTH

Like the springs that unite to form the headwaters of the Conecuh
River near Union Springs, Alabama, this series seeks to bring to-
gether the South's many traditions and cultures, celebrating at once
our differences and our commonality.

WADE HALL, SERIES EDITOR

ALSO IN THE CONECUH SERIES

The Outrageous Times of Larry Bruce Mitchell

Waters of Life from Conecuh Ridge: The Clyde May Story

It's Good Weather for Fudge: Conversing with Carson McCullers

THE CONECUH SERIES

FEAR NOT THE FALL

⇒ POEMS ⇐

AND

FANNIE LOU HAMER:
THIS LITTLE LIGHT . . .

⇒ A TWO-ACT DRAMA ⇐

BILLIE JEAN YOUNG

INTRODUCTION BY MARGARET ROSE GLADNEY

NEWSOUTH BOOKS

Montgomery

NewSouth Books
P.O. Box 1588
Montgomery, AL 36102

Library of Congress Cataloging-in-Publication Data
ISBN 1-58838-161-7

Design by Randall Williams
Printed in the United States of America

THE CONECUH SERIES

CELEBRATING DIVERSITY IN THE SOUTH

Like the springs that unite to form the headwaters of the Conecuh
River near Union Springs, Alabama, this series seeks to bring to-
gether the South's many traditions and cultures, celebrating at once
our differences and our commonality.

TO THE MEMORY OF MY SISTER-FRIENDS
WHO CROSSED OVER TO THE OTHER SIDE:

SANDRA LYNETTE SWANS, MY COSMIC TWIN

VIRGIA BROCK SHEDD

INGRID WASHINAWATOK

AND DANA ALSTON

Contents

Preface

WADE HALL

Reading the poems and the play in this collection by Billie Jean Young, you will begin hearing such distinct voices as Lorraine Hansberry, Zora Neale Hurston, Nikki Finney, Louise Clifton, Maya Angelou—even Gwendolyn Brooks, whom I once had the pleasure of hearing and interviewing. Young's voice, however, adds another color to this vivid rainbow of African American artists—all of them singing new songs in American writing. They all make vital, vibrant, arresting sounds.

Indeed, none of these earlier authors writes like Billie Jean Young because none of them has lived her life. She writes out of her own experiences, close to her skin and in an African-tinged Alabama accent as fresh, as original, as American as any of her predecessors. Perhaps even more than they, she can lay claim to being a new kind of Bardic voice, a direct, in-your-face, throbbing and sassy voice that is always genuine. It is as mythic as Africa and as up-to-date as Atlanta.

Expect to be surprised. She is shocking and funny, sacred and sacrilegious, scatological and elegant, and she is always daring the reader to take one more step with her. Her imagery is as familiar as a hoe or "mama's rubboard hands" and as distant as the ocean or Alexander the Great. She shapes human history and the English language to her uses and makes them conform to her vision. Her passion, conviction and eloquence are always shining through.

Like Walt Whitman, she sometimes shouts above the rooftops,

and like him, her vision can be egocentric. The poem he placed first in Leaves of Grass, "Oneself I Sing," announces his intention to explore the universe by exploring himself and a leaf of grass; likewise, Young celebrates herself in her first poem:

Who Me?
I just a Black beauty be,
All loose and free
And trying to be me.

Of course, like Whitman and all good poets her vision is personal and cosmic, and her poems range from a quick take like "I and My Shadow Have Not Always Gotten Along" to "Elmina Castle," an ambitious and haunting indictment of slavery. "Fannie Lou Hamer: This Little Light . . ." is a tribute to the human rights activist and a powerful dramatic presentation of the campaign for voter registration and its signature role in the civil rights movement. Moreover, in everything, Young not only speaks for herself but also for her sisters and brothers whose voices we have not heard.

In these words Whitman described the true American poet: "Each singing what belongs to him or her and none else," singing songs "Of Life immense in passion, pulse, and power." Knowingly or not, Billie Jean Young has answered his call.

Read her play and her poems and hear her painful and uplifting songs of aspiration and hope. We are proud to add her voice to the Conecuh Series, which celebrates a diverse choir of many voices.

Introduction

MARGARET ROSE GLADNEY

At first glance, Billie Jean Young's life may be read as a twentieth century American success story: She was born July 21, 1947, the fifth of seven children in a sharecropping family whose roots have been traced to slavery days in southwest Alabama's Choctaw County. Her formal education began in a rural one-room school and she graduated from an all-black public high school in 1964. A direct beneficiary of the 1960s civil rights movement, Young found her first opportunity for personal and professional growth at age twenty when she moved to Selma, Alabama, to work for the Southwest Alabama Farmer's Cooperative Association (SWAFCA), a cooperative formed by local civil rights activists to help low-income small farmers in ten west Alabama counties get a fair wage for their produce. During the seven years she worked for SWAFCA, Young helped found the Black Belt Arts and Cultural Center (BBACC), a community-based theater for rural youth through which, as its artistic director, she introduced black theater to Selma. While supporting herself and her two sons directing community theater and rural development projects in the 1970s, Young earned two degrees from two of Alabama's formerly all-white private colleges. Not only was she the first African American to graduate from Judson College for Women in Marion, Alabama, but her honors thesis, "The Evolution of the Black Hero in American Drama," earned her a B.A. with honors and with distinction. In 1979 she became the second African American woman to earn a law degree from Samford University's Cumberland School of Law.

Making a name for herself regionally in rural development work in the 1980s, she co-founded and directed the Southern Rural Women's Network (SRWN) before writing and producing her best known work: *Fannie Lou Hamer: This Little Light*, a one-woman play based on the life of the Mississippi Delta freedom fighter and human rights activist Fannie Lou Hamer. In recognition of her work in preserving the history of African American women through the play and for her organizing work through the SRWN, Young was named a 1984 MacArthur Fellow by the John D. and Catherine T. MacArthur Foundation. Young traveled widely in the 1980s and 1990s serving on the boards of national organizations concerned with rural women in community development projects and performing her play throughout the U.S. and in Ghana, China, Belize, and the Caribbean. While teaching in Jackson State University's Department of Speech and Dramatic Art from 1990 to 1996, Young extended her own dramatic roles beyond the stage to include television and film. In 1995 she was awarded the Mississippi Governor's Award for Artistic Achievement and the Lucy Prince Terry Unsung Heroine Award.

Billie Jean Young's poetry, however, reflects a life of struggle as well as affirmation. Her poetry honors the tradition of resistance she benefited from as a child even before she joined the economic justice organizations of the 1960s and 1970s. The tradition she dramatizes in her acclaimed portrayal of Fannie Lou Hamer—the tradition of making a way out of no way—is the same tradition she celebrates in remembering her mother's "rub-board hands." Her

---

Margaret Rose Gladney is Associate Professor Emeritus of American Studies at the University of Alabama, Tuscaloosa.

poetry also reveals the deeply painful, often hidden costs of living in a tradition of resistance, costs not readily apparent in her stellar resume of accomplishments and awards. In this collection Young celebrates her personhood as well as her African American womanhood and the power of self-creation and re-creation in the face of personal rejection, abuse, systemic exploitation and oppression. Organized chronologically with each section indicating a significant turning point in her adult life, her poems may be read as road markers from her life's journey. For Young, the road is not a freeway; it is not even always paved. It is, however, a familiar path and one any of us can enter.

Most of the poems in Section One were written between 1974 and 1980, the years during and immediately after Young attended law school in Birmingham, Alabama. Young has described those years in her late twenties and early thirties as "a time when the blunder of youth passes away and you have no one to blame but yourself."[1] Whether addressing personal or social relationships, as in "My Boys Are the Light of My Life," "I Will Give to You," or "My Name Is Black," the narrator in these poems consciously takes full responsibility for her own self-definition. Young entered law school with virtually no financial support from her family; indeed, they expected her to go to work and take care of her children rather than pursuing a law degree. With only a tuition scholarship, Young struggled to support herself by conducting dance and acting workshops five evenings a week in an inner-city community center and producing three main-stage performances a season with Birmingham's Black Fire Dance Company and Theatre. Young's identification with and appreciation for the talented young African-American women with whom she worked would inspire the poems "Black Beauty" and "Little African Princess." "The Child of Too," "I Know You," and "Damn Self" speak directly to the complex, frustrating, often painful experiences of negotiating the boundaries of race in a desegregating yet segregated world.

By the time she completed law school, Young had decided to pursue her interest in rural economic development and community theatre rather than the practice of law. In December 1977 she rejoined the community development movement in Alabama. Hired as research associate for program development and director of a legal services program for poor blacks with land problems, Young also developed and directed a community-based dance and theater program for African-American youth in the Branch Heights community in Greene County, Alabama. Through drama and dance she helped young people and their families address many of the legacies of poverty and racism that seemed to render them powerless. Young's leadership, however, was not always valued and supported within the power structure of the economic justice movement. The poems, "I Watch from Afar," I Spent Too Much Time Dreaming," and "The Spiral Staircase," reflect Young's sense of alienation and despair as she faced unacknowledged sexism in her work environment.

In 1979 Young reluctantly left Alabama to take a position as land specialist with Rural America's Rural Land Alliance in Washington, D.C. Promoted to Southeastern Region Associate Director in 1981, she hired as her assistant Julia Winn, with whom she had worked in Branch Heights; together they moved to Jackson, Mississippi, and launched the Southern Rural Women's Network (SRWN). Attracting educated, professional, as well as uneducated, poor and unemployed women from seven southeastern states, the first SRWN conference theme, "Isn't It About Time Someone Spoke Up for Rural women?" reflected Young's experience with civil rights and anti-poverty organizations. "Rural black women had organized through churches and sororities, but they had never organized to address discrimination as women and as black people," Young noted. "We dealt so much with racism during the civil rights movement we didn't recognize sexism."[2] Although the conference organizers encountered some accusations of male-bashing, the conferees applauded and cheered when Young read her "Hoeing/Whoring" poems candidly referencing her own childhood experiences with sexual assault and racism and the resulting expressions of self-hate and internalized oppression she had witnessed in herself and other rural African-American women's personal relationships.

The poems in Section Two were written between 1983 and 1995, the years when Young traveled widely as director of the Southern Rural Women's Network and in connection with her service on the boards of Agricultural Missions and the Rural Development Leadership Network. Reflecting Young's position as a spokesperson for the concerns of rural African-American women, these poems address the globally destructive impact of systemic racism and sexism in America's international as well as domestic policies. From a more personal perspective, the poems "Introductions" and "Elmina Castle" expand themes of self-definition and affirmation addressed in earlier poems such as "My Name is Black" and "Children of the Motherland": the importance of acknowledging and defining the narrator's present as well as historical relationship to other African peoples. The affirming voice of the resilient, proud, first African in the New World endures precisely because she keeps herself in view and refuses to forget the anguished screams of the abandoned, abused daughter sold into slavery from Elmina Castle.

Many of the poems in "Voluntary Voyages" reflect Young's experiences in the Central American country of Belize, where she lived in the late 1980s and to which she frequently returns. In celebration of International Women's Day in March of 1985, the Belize Rural Women's Association and the Belize Organization for Women and National Development sponsored three performances of Young's *Fannie Lou Hamer: This Little Light*. Young felt especially welcome in Dangriga, a town in southern Belize where the population is largely Garifuna, a mixture of African and Carib Indian peoples. "But for the palm trees and beautiful ocean," she would later write, "Dangriga could have been a town in the rural United States." Although practically no one there had heard of Fannie Lou Hamer and Young worried that they would not understand Hamer's deep Southern accent, she found their reception to her performance "one of the greatest communication experiences of [her] life." Like Hamer and herself, Young realized, the Dangrigans were "speaking some variation of somebody else's language."[3] The poetry Young would write in Belize reflects her keen ear and love for the Garifuna, their land, and their language. She would return to live and work in Dangriga not only because she felt at home there but also because she appreciated and needed its difference. "African Americans need to go somewhere and see Africans in charge," Young explains. "It's very hard to understand and try to rid yourself of the weight of racism while living in [the United States]. You don't even know that you have it until you leave the country, get rid of it, and come back and feel it again."[4] The playful narrator in "Bridgefoot" exemplifies the poet's liberated voice, the age-old freedom of the outside/insider to observe and comment on the culture's unique yet human foibles.

In 1996 Young returned to live in her hometown of Pennington, Alabama, ostensibly to care for her mother, but also to live more fully on her own terms rather than those of institutions and foundations. Many called her a fool, or worse, for leaving her tenure-track professor's pay at Jackson State University and resigning her positions of influence on the boards of national agencies to be true to her gut and follow her dreams. The narrator's candid affirmation of her relationship to her mother and her own childhood in "Mama's Rub-board Hands" indicates the shifts in subject and tone that prevail in Section Three. "Five Decades of Living" may be read as a mid-life memoir in which Young expands the reflective assessment of her life beyond childhood to include lessons she wants to pass on to succeeding generations. Written initially as letters to a friend and sister poet, Kathy Engel, the last three poems continue the mid-life reflections. Across racial, regional, and class differences, Young challenges her friend and herself to "fear not the fall" as writers and women, and to speak truth about their own lives and the lives of other women who died in the struggle to live free. Taken as a whole, the poems in this section leave no doubt that Young's struggle for liberation and self-determination continues. If in the poetry of her thirties Young determined to be her "damn self," to value the black woman-child, her body, her self-expression, and her independence, in the poetry of her fifties she pledges to continue the struggle to make a place where she can live and create, where she can love and support herself and her community.

---

[1] Billie Jean Young to Rose Gladney, July 2002. Correspondence in possession of author.

[2] Billie Jean Young to Women in the South class, University of Alabama, March 2000.

[3] Billie Jean Young, "This Little Light of Mine: Dramatizing the Life of Fannie Lou Hamer," in eds. Joanne M. Braxton and Andree Nicola McLaughlin, *Wild Women in the Whirlwind: Afra-American Culture and the Contemporary Literary Renaissance* (Rutgers University Press: 1990), 143.

[4] Interview with Billie Jean Young, Pennington, Alabama, June 1998, in possession of author.

FEAR NOT THE FALL

⇒ POEMS ⇐

SECTION 1

CHILD OF TOO

BLACK BEAUTY

Who? Me?
I just a Black beauty be,
all loose and free
and trying to be me.

Society ladies see me coming,
shake they heads in disgust.
Now the society men,
they something else again.
They see me coming and raise up a fuss.
OOOOOOHHH, weee! Sho nuff!

Counselor sent me to the charm school,
wanted me to learn how to walk and talk.
"Don't bounce up and down,
don't shake when you walk,
Don't open your mouth
keep it closed when you talk."
Who? me? I just a Black beauty be.
All loose and free,
and trying to be me.

Told me lately down at the school,
don't be no fool:
bat your eyes, flutter your lids,
drop your hanky, let the gentleman bid.
Who? Me?
I just a Black beauty be.
All loose and free, and trying to be me.

Done tried so hard to be Miss Prim,
worked so hard 'til my head hurt.
I can't be Miss Prim
when I be me.
It ain't a part of my real personality.
Who? me? I just a Black beauty be,
All loose and free
and GOTS to be me.

LITTLE AFRICAN PRINCESS

Little African Princess,
you bewilder me,
as much as I love you,
I can write no poems for you.
Oh, I've had the inspiration,
God knows the inclination,
but every time I start,
this uncontrollable heart
of mine fills up with the beauty of you,
and I can make no poem of you.

Methought one day, off with yourself,
get your brains off the shelf,
surely words are but hand tools
in the poet's craft and must be used—Create!

And, oh, my wayward pen
I wish you could see,
running, scribbling, flying,

across pages two or three,
but, ah, no poems do I create,
no odes do I make,
fit to capture the essence of you.
(I can't even finish a poem about not being able
to finish a poem about you!)

You are the sunshine of summers yet to come,
you are the beginning of the outcome,
and therein lies the key:

You write it better than me,
you add a new verse everyday,
just living, loving, giving, dancing,
laughing, loving, crying,
Being your own delightful self.
(I'm gonna put this paper and pen down
and let you write your own poems
across the Pages of Time.)

My Boys Are the Light of My Life

Keith
Keith, my rebel child,
You make me laugh even as I cry
While giving me pain and pleasure
and in good measure,
A wholesome, big-hearted lad you are
like I wanted to be
You are my rebel side, the side that's hidden inside of me.

Anthony
Anthony Dwayne, born on the street that bears your name:
Child of my childhood—my first one—
I never got over you—too much of me are you;
My son/my brother/my serious side, that gets the best of me.

My Name Is Black

One time a man,
an African man,
nappy headed man,
asked me my name.
Told him my name
and a lot more I told
to that African man
who asked me my name:

My name is the part of me that is
Negro and American
nappy headed woman that I am,
the color of my skin is the part of me
that was stolen,
and belongs with my name.

Now the other part of me,
which is all of me that is woman,
is midnight Black and African.

My name is Black.

Mother's Children

When children of the Motherland
meet and greet each other,
time and circumstance are suspended:

Continents merge,
while oceans fight to control themselves,
the hyena cackles—admiringly.

Mother's children must learn each other,
each one, Sister and Brother.

You Must Be How Tenderness Feels

You must be how tenderness feels
the rhythm of it,
different this time,
gently, tenderly.

Going and coming
with each other,
and finally arriving—
together.

Like two old autumn leaves plastered together, swaying gently
'gainst the breeze, waiting for winter to claim them.

I WILL GIVE TO YOU

I will give to you
Only so much as I would
Wish you to have of me,
Without receipt or acknowledgment . . .

After that, you begin to
take, or steal—
And I don't like that.

HOEING I

Folks always want you to do their hoeing for them.
Even when I was just a little girl
Miss Ellen wanted me to do her hoeing for her.
Wasn't enough that I was her child's playmate,
Wasn't enough that me and Nita played together
every day in the sand building sand castles
Capturing cow ants and fencing them in and getting stung
Wasn't enough for me to be Nita's friend
Miss Ellen wanted me to be her hoe girl too.

Put a hoe in my hand, yes she did
Every day when it was evening time
when the sun moved out the top of
the sky and lunch was over,
Miss Ellen would call Nita for her nap.
And it was then she put the hoe in my hand.
I started at the age of 7 doing Miss Ellen's hoeing for her.

And I was too little.
But I hoed anyway 'cause it seemed that's
what I was supposed to do.

It might have gone on forever
But one day Miss Ellen got to feeling guilty I reckon and
fooled around and gave me a quarter.
I rushed home with my shiny new quarter proud as I could be
and Mama allowed as to why Miss Ellen was giving me money.
And I told her Miss Ellen had me hoeing for her.
Mama didn't say nothing but it was a long time before
I got to see Nita again.
And then she had to come see me
When I came down with the whooping cough.
I still don't know what happened but
The next time Miss Ellen called Nita in for her nap,
She looked at me and said: "And Billie Jean, you
come on inside too, 'cause your mama don't want you
in the sun."

Mama musta got Miss Ellen told!

Hoeing/Whoring II

And while we was still young, we learned that lots of folks like
for young girls to whore for them:

Wasn't but three girls in my neighborhood and we all knew
what Mr. Shelly Parkingson did to Bessie Mae King
back in 1956 when we was all about eight years old
and our folks hired us out to him to pick his field peas,
'cause Miss Edwina said she got freckles and sunburn if she
worked in the field.
Mr. Shelly took Bessie Mae off to that little house up in the field
and had his way with her. Gave her a dollar, told her it was
easy money, and told her not to tell anybody.

He being a no-count, low-down trashy old man,
he told Bessie Mae to take her clothes off and lay down on the
dirty mattress.
Told her he wasn't going to hurt her,
just took his clothes off and spilled some sticky nasty stuff
all over her and then licked it off.
And Bessie Mae was too shame and didn't tell nobody but us
about Mr. Parkingson making her whore for him, back in 1956,
'til 22 years later when she ran smack dab into the face of
a nervous breakdown, looked it in the eye, and decided
she better tell somebody about herself,
and turned around and ran to get some therapy
for her emotions.
Since then, she finally figured out why she was hopping in and
outta bed with white men even though she hated them anyway,
just so she could keep on degrading herself and punishing herself
for something a no-good, sick cracker did to her when she was 8.

White folks still had Bessie Mae whoring and she wasn't even getting a mink coat and diamond rings like the movie stars when they whore around with white men.

Bessie Mae say she aint into whoring no more . . . for either white or black men,

Which brings me to a most unmentionable subject:
Some time ago, we three made the personal decision that we was tired of whoring and hoeing for Black men, too.

Whoring Whores III

We tired-a coming home from work to get slapped up side the head by a unemployed Nigger who moved in
'cause you felt sorry for him.
And you buy his story and a pair of pants for him, too,
when you cash your paycheck on Friday
or when the ADC check come on the 11th,
so he can look all spiffy when he step out on you tonight,
and when he drags back in Sunday morning, with a bad attitude
'cause some chick done took all that he didn't gamble away
at the Dog Track, and a bad headache from sitting around
pulling on too many home-grown joints trying to get high,
complaining 'cause you ain't cooked breakfast yet,
you'll be satisfied. You'll wash the stains out of your pants
bought with your money
and as you lovingly fold the polyester crease back in them
and hit them with the iron a time or two,
you'll convince yourself that you like whoring for your man.

Whoring your dignity and self respect away in order to keep
a no-count Nigger in your bed,
who gone walk off on you anyhow
soon as one of your children come down for a extended stay in
the hospital, or one of your daughters needs $200 for
an abortion and the little money get tighter and you ain't got
so much time no more to be giving him attention, 'cause you
worried about your child;
Or if you're lucky and your children stay healthy
and you up and have to have a hysterectomy or your
gall bladder removed
(it don't really make no difference which one),
the Nigger get it in his head that you ain't the same no more.
He gone walk off anyhow.
After all, this was only intended to be a short,
no-strings-attached-visit.
He been looking for a way to get out,
so he can find somebody new and exciting to whore for him.
You were beginning to get a little dull.
And you done got so used to it,
you just hump up in your shoulders,
and go out and buy you a new red jumpsuit,
and make it down to the Black Lite Lounge on Saturday night
and find you somebody else to whore for.
It ain't too hard, they lined up out there.
Pretty boys, ugly ones, the big muscled and the small waisted,
even the round bottom closet queens
who'll fool around with you anyhow,
and let you whore for them too,
cause they need the "respectability" of associating with a female.
And you let them move in with you,
sometimes with their other men.

And sit around your living room and drink beer
and watch the soaps while you work,
and rape your daughter or sometimes your son,
and turn her on to coke and pot
so she can get all hot and bothered
and ready for them.
And you knew from the start
that this was just another two month,
two week, two day no-strings-attached mess of an affair;
and this time you ain't even getting your money's worth.

Why you continue to whore, Whore?

My Symphony

There was a lilt somewhere in there, in that love of ours.
I know. I heard the melody long before you did.

And I remembered it and emphasized upon the theme. Added a
new note here and there, no Master Plan, just playing it by ear,
the way my heart told me I should hear—and hear I did!

I HEARD A SYMPHONY.
Conducted by some famous German,
I guess—musta been.
And I had myself a listening good time—while it lasted.
The symphony, I mean.

Sometimes I could hear the brass street band playing in the
background of the symphony I was listening to, trying to drown

it out; a bit disconcerting I must admit, but always there was my symphony anyway to overpower it and give sweet reassurance to my willing ears.

I thought so, at least.

I didn't know. I thought you heard the symphony, too. Don't know why. Just assumed you did.

No Pieces for Me

Don't want no piece of a man no more.
Got to have me a whole man or nothing at all.
You say I live in a dream world?
got my head sticking in the sand?
there's got to be more than a piece of a man somewhere.
This is America land.

Tired of playing with papier mache,
putting together pieces like paper dolls,
some strength here, a little change there,
a mind in Alabama and my juices down in Louisiana.

My arms too tired to be reaching 'round all over the place,
gathering up itty-bitty quilt pieces
to patch up me some kinda man.
Too much strain on my eyes,
sorting out, trying to match up pieces,
too hard on my fingers sewing and mending
sometimes groping in the dark
trying to put me a man together

when he got six different heads
scattered all over the place.
My feet tired a running to rummage sales,
hunting for scraps and remnants
leftovers,
used-to-be's.

Don't really care if he comes out of the basement of Filene's
at bargain basement prices,
just so he's worth more,
a good deal more,
for me.
A whole already-put-together store bought man
with all the parts assembled
is what I want.
Been doing without him too long now,
ain't gone make do no more wit no pieces.
I want the whole hog or nothing at all!

They Don't Come

When they say, "I'll be there,"
they put you off for another day.
They don't come.
They don't care.

They don't come to you when
you wish they would.
Nor answer the phone when
you need to talk.

Or send flowers when
you're depressed.
Or bring you to laughter when
you're in tears.
They don't come.

They stay away—the other way,
clear of tears and depression,
and the desire to talk in schizoid conversation.

They just don't come.

CJ and EJ, they don't come
Mama and Dead Papa, they don't come
nor siblings,
nor cousins once removed.
They don't come.

I came.
By myself, thus far.
In bad times.

If you see me when times are better,
don't be alarmed,
write me a letter.
Just don't come.

I Know You

I know you.
I know you better than you know me,
I started first grade with you.
Oh, you didn't ever see me.
I saw you all the time.

In my Black school that was curiously yours,
I saw you.
Hiding in my first grade reader,
jumping rope, skipping along with Tip,
going uphill to look for water,
and calling yourself Jack and Jill,
Dick and Jane, and Tom and Jerry,
with your crew cut hair and your yellow ponytail,
I saw you.
Coming 'round the mountain when you come,
driving six white horses when you come,
I saw you.

I saw you
jumping out of my filmstrips in my sex education class,
grinning at me from my posters
that told me how to comb my hair,
brush my teeth, and take a bath,
and use a Kleenex when I sneeze.
I saw you.

And I got to know you,
better than I know me,
and better than you know me,

I know you.

I never saw myself.

THE CHILD OF TOO

I go through changes
because of me and who I am
and because of you
and who you are.
I am the Child of Too.

My skin is always a shade too—
too light,
too dark,
too yellow,
too brown,
too bright,
It is almost never just right.

My name is too common,
my speech is too informal,
my lips are too thick,
my feet are too big,
my hips are too wide,
But, I am your child.

I am the Child of Too,
too much
too little

too late
The Child of Too
I am.
One of you whom I never met.
I make no apologies for you.
I make no apologies for me
for I must go on.

Back there in my past—
dark or light
high or low
narrow or wide—
I can't account for you.
I make the best of me
even with my Too,
And from two too's
I try to make one—
Me!

Damn Self

I'm gonna be my damn self.
I'm gonna fill up a bucketful of me
and let it overflow all over the place,
spill all over this whitewashed world,
full of lies and hate.
Maybe it'll help to clean up some of this slime
that's causing me to keep on tripping up
and falling down.
And I ain't filling out no more forms for you

with pencils and pen and futility,
writing away my life on paper
smeared with my blood
and my fingerprints.

I'm gonna be my damn self.
And I ain't sugar coatin' my speech for you
no more to sit around and pick my brain
and try to figure out my psyche,
and pull up you a chair,
and rare back
and prop up your feet at night
and say:
"Oh, I conquered me a Nigger today.
Let me tell you what she say:

'Oh, please, Mr. Man and Miss Ann,
please try to understand
that I is jest a little colored person
what reached too high.
I didn't mean to insult y'all
and do y'all stuff better
than y'all could do it.
That's what y'all mad about, ain't it?'

See, I let you inta my house
and my various homes
and around my friends and family
and now you think you know me.
I let you see us relax
and communicate with each other
and you even had the privilege

of hearing my dialect
as I relaxed with my friends
and bar-b-qued ribs
and made potato salad
and cole slaw sometimes
and listened to Black music
and got up and danced
if we felt like it
and then just relax some more
in our Blackness—
I let you in on all that.
And you shook your head
up and down, and said,
"Good. Prime candidate,
add this one to the slate."

And I was so flattered,
and so pleased
cause I thought you wanted me
and you thought so, too.
But you don't know me,
well as you think you do.
You got to exposing me
and giving me opportunity.
And I started to taking me
some opportunity,
and sounding like you do—
sounding like you do—
and doing what you do—
and doing it better than you.
You taught me to imitate well, didn't you?
And you didn't 'preciate it,

'cause it started to
conflicting with you,
making me visible
and putting me in history,
and finding me in history
where I was buried,
creating conflicts for you,
with your superior self.

So you convinced Bakke and Defunius 'nem
that something was inherently evil
in allowing me a chance to do my thing.
And Bakke convinced the Supreme Court
of this whole Newninted States
that I was evil and unconstitutional,
 standing in the doorway
of white folks education
and that po' little ole me
could keep Bakke from being a doctor
if he wanted to.
And they bought it.
And the rest of the country did, too
and we got proposition 13
and 14 and 15
all over the world
even in Britain
where stony faced Margaret Thatcher
is running good,
and done won
on a conservative ticket
of proposition 13s
and keeping non-Europeans

from immigrating to Britain,
closing off the doors.

I was doing my thing too well
and y'all got hip
and started to closing off the doors
trying to put me in a room by myself
so nobody could see me,

Used to be, every time
y'all started closing off them doors
I started changing faces in there
fixing myself up
(And you harder to suit
than any overseer ever I did see)
I don't even cuss in my poetry!
In the privacy of darkness
'midst near lethal doses
of inbred propaganda,
I started changing into me a new face
every time,
trying to please you.

Anyway, y'all started to closing off them doors
just as quick as y'all could
when people started to assert themselves
and made some of y'all's progress.
Well, I ain't got no more faces
for you.
I'm gonna be my damn self!

I Watch from Afar

I watch from afar
as things collapse
and try not to position myself
at the bottom of the heap
Though sometimes I fail
and wind up there anyway

I Spent Too Much Time Dreaming

I spent too much time
Dreaming far away dreams
And not appreciating
the dream I was living
til I had a nightmare
one day
And woke up and realized
I was awake already.

The Spiral Staircase

On the way up the Spiral Staircase
I lost my balance, took a step back—
halted momentarily
and surveyed the terrain.

Seeing rockiness beneath me
and jutting boulders at the top of my head
I waited a while longer,
suspended, as it were
in the moist mid air of indecision

To move on?

SECTION 2

VOLUNTARY VOYAGES

You Bettah Belize It!

Belize is a morning sunrise
fresh on the horizon
Belize is sunshine
aflame in the sky,
shimmering, shuddering,
aquiver with desire.

Belize is the prettiest little place
on the face
of the earth.
Garden of Eden rediscovered.
You bettah Belize it
because now you see it
now you don't
and you bettah not tink I kidding either.

The mangoes do fall hard atop
a manmade roof
and wake a woman or man
out of a sound siesta.
"Eat the domn ting, Mon!"
How cruel to be awakened from so sound a sleep!
To what, for whom?

Belize is a sleeping virgin
lying belly up
with legs askew
You bettah wake up, gal,
somebody will rape you!

Belize is a small uncut jewel.
Who will wield the jeweler's tool?
Who deigns to reshape perfection?

I and My Shadow
Have Not Always Gotten Along

Today I make footprints
on the path,
come back
after my visit and tea
and find my tracks
there, upon the road,
the imprint of me
un-erased.
I stroll along,
happy to see myself:
I and my shadow
who have not always gotten along.

Facing the Caribbean Sea

It is to the East
I face the day
another day of
remembrances
and silent
recriminations
and sorrow

for loyalty misplaced
for trust unearned
given too freely
and greedily consumed.

Trust, once broken,
can never be perfectly repaired
neither can a broken heart.
Mended maybe.
But not just like before.

At Water's Edge

On the verge
of the sea,
halfway to being an island
sits Belize
at water's edge.
Amidst war and turmoil
in a region so beset
Belize rests,
sitting
at water's edge.
A haven for the weary
refuge for the worn
who roam
in search of a home
Belize waits
at water's edge.

I wait
midst scattered debris
at water's edge.

At water's edge
I face a vast
and uncompromising horizon
at water's edge
I see afar
the wonder I live
at water's edge.
I await some sign
of cleansing
of revelation
at water's edge.

BRIDGEFOOT

I Bridgefoot
I sit at the Bridgefoot
I hear evil
see evil
and yes,
sometimes it is necessary for me
to speak evil.
Sittin' on the Bridgefoot the way I do
I have plenty chance to put two and two together
lotta times when nobody else noticin'
I sittin' there just a countin', see?

putting two and two together.

Disinformation:

Garinagu
are more Indian
than African.
which Indian?
Any Indian.
See!
See how they love to fish!
How they swing machete!
Noble creatures they,
never so African
as Indian.
See the healing rituals—
See the ceremonies
never African!
The teacher say:
"The African didn't keep anything on American shores;
they were slaves,
and when they stopped being slaves,
they tried to forget."

Funny.
How they didn't forget
their rhythms
their dances
their colors
their language
the gait of their walk
the tilt of their head:

the Africans kept that much
even if they are Indians!

Belize,
picture perfect
land of sun
and sea.
Don't focus!
Kodak can only
mess it up!
Belize is
a picture!
And if you can't buy it inna States, gial,
It can't be bought.
I going dere for me next V-cation,
you know.
Me dah-tah, she di send for me.

Do you know the way to San Jose?
Even in Belize
California is identified as some kind of jail,
albeit by the sea.
Hang on, Snoopy,
Snoopy, hang on.

Arab said that he heard
that a certain fella
not from we Belize
poured a glass of red Kool-Aid
all over the gal
teaching here
from the Modder Country

and he got suspended from he teaching job
Wonder what that was all about?

I Bridgefoot
I sit at the bridgefoot
I hear evil
see evil
and yes, sometimes
it is necessary for me to
speak evil.

I mean this is live shit!

The soldiers stop the bus
in Honduras
and wake you up
to write your name
in their notebook.
In Belize,
the police stop the bus
on the way from Dangriga
and going back in:
QUARANTINE!
MEDITERRANEAN FRUIT FLY
MAY BE IN DANGRIGA
DO NOT BRING FRUITS FROM DANGRIGA/
STANN CREEK!
But Stann Creek
is the citrus valley.
Me Mangoes! dey de rot up!
Me gwine a poor house!

Police search the bus
and can only find
two heads of cabbage
double head cabbage
which they took off the bus
and then put back on.
In retaliation,
they searched the knapsack
of the only Dread Brother
'pon the bus
and sent the bus on down
into the Stann Creek Valley
descending
into the land
of too ripe mangoes
headed fast
to becoming fertilizer—
all lines to the valley
choked dry,
cut off
by the Mediterranean fruit fly.

It being one of those dull dull weeks
when everybody sittin' around
waiting
on something to happen.
Over two weeks and nobody to wake
no nine night in sight,
de last family Mass well nigh forgot about.
Pickney gone to school,
Caye wander over to the bar in Harlem Square,
find Peter nursing bitters at the bar,

no merriment,
no rum,
no nine night to talk 'bout.
Caye say: Nobody dead lately.
Peter nod he head:
No nine night in sight.

Den the church bell rung out.
Silence in the bar:
Caye could hear the roaches crawling
along the bar,
hear Billy the bartender and Peter
breathing.
In point of fact,
you could hear a rat pee on cotton.
Caye say: da who da bell dat?
Peter say: da you!
Caye say: Somebody done dead!
Peter say: Wake tonight.
Caye say: Yeah, nine night probably fall on a weekend.
Peter say: Somebody dead lately.
De bar come alive.
Drink to de dear departed.
Billy smile.
I mean this is live!

Caye say woman behind him on the bus
say to Caye in Garifuna,
cause she know Caye's wife can't unnerstand, see?
"You let your woman sit between two men?"
Caye look around,
see the Kulture Keeper,

lady who teach inna high school,
Caye so sure she no talk to he,
Caye say he say: Excuse me?
Kulture Keeper repeat the same ting.
Caye say he say,
in he best deep freeze voice:
"Free people sit where they wish."
Kulture Keeper toss she jeri curled head, say: Shuh!
Caye smile. Knocked all the words outta she!

Caye say anodder time
anodder Kulture Keeper
sashay up to he:
"You let you wife wear shorts!"
Caye say he bristle:
"You di like me wife shorts or not?"
Kulture Keeper say: "What?"
"You heard me. You like me wife shorts or not?"
Caye know dere ain't no safe teef anser to he question, see?
"I mean, you see, culturally . . . "
Caye cut he off again:
Naw, mon, answer me. You de one wit you mouth all over me
wife's body. Answer me! You di bring it up!"
The Kulture Keeper running away all de time!
I mean I get this on bridgefoot
straight down the line! Live!

INTRODUCTIONS

(or Plea from a Black American)
?Me llama?
(My name?)
Me llama no es Americana.
Me llama es Negra.
(My name is Black)
Entonces, yo soy Americana.
Never before.
You not know difference, mon?
Wait!
Me tell you.

First,
there is the First American,
which I am not,
though that is my sister, too,
as quiet as it is kept.
I am the first African
in the New World,
treading upon new soil,
making a new race
on a new continent,
being called by new names
like Phyllis and George;
being called out of my name,
like Americana and Knee-grow.

I am the first African
brought to North American shores,
tongue cut out,

I fashioned a new language:

A new dance.
Out of the old came new,
new rhythms, jazz, blues;
new songs, hymns, dirges;
new conversation.
In short, I adapted.
I took my African self
and gave rhythm to dissonance,
named my children King and Prince
Colonel and Major
to replace titles violently snatched away
in the New World.
Resilient was I, creative.
I even made a word for white: Buckra!
Laughed at my own absurdities,
resolved my conflicts as best I could,
adjusted to the paleness that crept through.
And even though
angel food cake is white
and devil food cake is black,
a white lie is the truth
and anything black devastatingly oppressive
as in :

blackmail
black list
black market
black eye
and so forth
and so on,

I still remembered
that I am the first African in the New World
and held on to myself,
though sometimes it was hard.
Sometimes I could not see myself
behind a facade of Mona Lisa smiles
hanging on my walls
and Smurfs painted on my cradle
riding Yankee Doodle to town
with Mickey Mouse holding the reins,
not me.

Though sometimes it was hard to see myself,
yet, I kept myself in sight.
I am the first African
in the New World.
Not ashamed of my bandana/ed head
nor my kinky locks.
I admire my broad bare feet,
the better to plant wide hips upon.
Of them, I am proud
and balanced.

I walk not upon tippy toes,
I plant my feet upon the road,
incline my head,
and I'm as good as there.

I ride for the sake of the auto
to grace its bald tinniness
with the solo that is me,
I need it not.

My feet are soil.
Look for me.
I am the rainbow.
You will find me everywhere:

In creamy hues of mocha
I come,
blueberry,
mahogany
midst high yellows
and browns, ebony
tan, reds,
black as the night,
and light, bright, almost white,
I come.
The African.
The first one.

I am the African who built the New World,
who picked the cotton and tilled the field,
cooked the food and raised the farm.
I am the African who slaved in Alabama
so industry could grow in New York.
 I am the African
on whose back the New World was built.
I am the African
whose black breasts performed double duty
to nurse my own
and others, too.
A suckling haven was I
for the asp that continuously poisoned me.

Yet,
I endured
this far.
Through this,
I have come
presenting myself to you.
Do you know me?
I am Negra.
Do you see me, mon?
Me tink not.
Do you love me, mon?
Me know not.
To know me is to love me.
?Se llama?
What is your name?

ELMINA CASTLE

I walked thru valleys,
my step uncertain,
o'er hill and dale I came
to get to you,
Elmina Castle—slave castle.

I traversed seas,
time, space, and place,
millennia of the mind,
to get back to you.

Uncertain voyages

to face the New World—unfree.
400 years
to return—
on an uncertain voyage
to face the old world—
voluntarily.

I survived!
I survived!

Afrika!
Africa.
I meet you at home
eye to eye
face to face
on these shores
I left so long ago.
Ago?
Ago when? Where?
"THIS is the place that the Lord hath made."

This is the place that the LORD hath made!

God, speak to me,
words I can hear,
drown out the sound
of my wailing voice,
my aching heart.
Ayieee...Ayiee!!!! Ayieeee!!
No, No, No!
Do you know the slave Girl?
Slave Girl.

Slave Girl?

Africa, speak to me.
of times past, rivers, oceans, storms on the Atlantic.
Quiet the storm in me.
Still the waters.
Say a prayer for me and mine.
Invoke, pray. I plead with you this day.

Your blues ain't like mine!

Mine eyes have seen the places, spaces,
hearts and minds
of the oppressors,
and my heart bleeds for you, Africa.

Mother Africa,
where are your children?
What did you say to them?
What did you do with them?
What words have you for me?
Aiyeeeeee! Aiye.e.e.eeeeeeeeee!

Let me find solace in your long, black, slender arms,
nurture me with nectar. Comfort me.
I bring back the seeds of your dishonor.
Your children are haunting you today—this day.
The ghosts of slavery are everywhere.
Perhaps the ghosts will answer?
Where is the witch lady?
(The wizard I cannot trust)
Speak to me,

borne away on the waves of a vast sea,
struggling in a ship's hold.
Did I survive?
I survived?
To cross back over. The ghost of your past,
returned to haunt these spaces, places,
ignoble, ignored, human cargo,
thing for sale.
Where were you, Mother Africa?
Mother?
Mother, the Great Stone got to move.
The Spirit speaks but I cannot hear,
tongue silenced to be replaced with Babel.
How can I build on the past with Babble?
Babel in my ear?
Where is thy temple,
O Great Mother of the world?
Where are your children?
How can I love you?
What is thy name? What is MY name?
Ashanti? Fanti? Speak to me! Answer me!
I am the spirit of the rebellious slave girl,
shoved through the hole.
I am the girl sold
for good teeth and proper breasts.
I am the one.
Look at me.
Look 'pon me and be ashamed.
Not of me, but BECAUSE of me, Mother.

Mother, what place hast thou prepared for me?
Give me rivers, let me dream dreams.

Spare me your disdain for the milk that taints my skin.
Allow me to be, to love, to honor thee.
Give me reason to smile,
to embrace,
to grab hold of your legs, to clutch at your skirts.
(Don't try to walk away, or I will trip you up—
holding on as I am.)
Mother, I need nurture. I must thrive.
I must feed upon your beautiful, black breasts
that continue to serve everyone but me.

I am the slave child.
Do not make me invisible.
Do not be ashamed of me.
Spare me your condescending.
Spare me your benign neglect.
I have come home,
the ghost of your past,
to confront you,
to confront myself—me—
the elders, and all the ancestors them.
I have come home.
Spare me.

Spare me!
I'm sorry, but your blues ain't like mine:
I traversed the deep,
arose to shake off the shackles of oppression,
ignorance and blind neglect.
Where are you? Aiyee! Aiyee?

Mother?

Ma?
Mudder?
Mu Dear?
MAMA?
I called out to you and silence answered me back.
The echo was louder than I could make it.
It was the best medicine—
laughterrrrrrrrrrrrrrr!

Mother, where are you?
I am the fetus aborted,
left somewhere in the trash
upon the garbage heap of humanity.
I found myself away from sustenance,
a dumping ground for the invaders, slave traders,
garbage men of the world
who create new races with your children.

Rape!
Rape!
I cried out to you and you did not hear, mother.
Mother, did my cries get lost
on the howling winds of the Atlantic,
and in the swaying palms on the shore?
Did I know better? Did you?

Mother! Speak to me. Embrace me.
I come in tears to roam the dungeons of the past,
the deep recesses of the soul and souls I left behind,
drowned in the Middle Passage.
What can you say to me?
The part of me that is you, Africa, AfriKAN?

Speak to me.

I am the slave girl come back to haunt you,
to wander among spirits for the rest of eternity—
without a proper place
in the wilderness across the Atlantic
with no place to call home.
Answer me, Mama!

WHERE ARE ALL THE COLORED MEN?

The world is at war,
does anybody care?
Somebody is leading us headlong into war
and the new unemployment line
is the draft office—
for the colored men
and even the yellow line got long
and winding and inattentive,
and Uncle Sam closed his hands
over his chest
and said, "Enough colored men."
So it's off to the prison cell,
by way of the street corner
and pimp talk
and pushing a little something—anything
to put a few coins in his pocket,
selling whatever is handy
wrap his mama up in a sheet
and sell her for white—

selling everything in sight.

Colored boys standing on street corners
in Knoxville, Tennessee,
little miniature Mafia men
pushing dope right in the middle of the projects,
hand it over to the customers bold
so all the ladies sitting on their steps
trying to keep cool in the bricks can see it
and know
that Little Big Man
selling dope in the middle of the kids'
marble game is tough.
He playing for keeps-
too tough to die.
But not too tough to go to prison and rot.
Yes, die a slow tortuous death
midst other dead, dying colored men
who don't know what happened either.

The War Poem I

My sons will fight no wars in AfriKA
Not for you, Uncle Sam.
My sons will shoot down no AfriKANS
in the name of AmeriKA. No!
My sons will not slaughter AfriKANS in Libya
nor Nicaragua. No!
We will not bear the blood on our hands
nor our children's children on theirs

in payment for sins committed
in the bush battle playground jungles
of silver haired generals and old cowboys in AmeriKA
who call the shots that kill colored boys
in jungles around the world.
No!
My sons will fight no AmeriKAN wars on anybody's soil.
NO!!!OOOOOHHHHHHHH!

The War Poem II

Ronald Reagan dropping
BOMBZ on AfriKa.
Hold up, Hold up!
Stop!
What you doing, Mr. Man?
Don't you know
who's in AFRIKA?
You can't drop no bomb
in Africa.
Can you?
Kin you?
You kin?
You can't
CanNot!
You did!
Hear ye, hear ye!
Sons and Daughters
of AFRIKA!
Ronald Reagan dropping

BOMBZ
on AFRIKA-A-A-A-A-A-AHHH!

Boy Is That You?

P'Nut, is that you
I don't know whether
it is you or not
'cause every Mother's
son
is you.
Every breathing,
living, dying
boy I see on the tv
is you.
Is that you
underneath the
debris and dirt
and sand
and desert sun?
I see the tv war
and I wonder:
P'Nut is that you?
I hear a voice on the telephone
far away
yet so near,
my heart quickens.
P'Nut, P'Apostrophe Nut, is that you?

Do you see me

in your mind's eye
from underneath
your helmet
and gas mask?
What do you see?
What do you feel?
P'Nut, is that you
I see a column of
tanks in the newspaper
and they say that it
is the first AD
Is that you?

Yes, you say,
it is I.
I live, I am,
I talk,
I speak,
I see
too much.
I know you see
too much
for anybody's eye to see.
I know you feel too much
for anybody to feel.
I know you know too much
for anybody to know.
Where are you?
Laughter.
Manly, boy laughter:
"I am in Saudi Arabia,"
you say

with a boyish laugh
bold, brave laugh
meant to allay
my fears.
Are you all right?
"Yes, I am fine,"
you say.
So near
so far away.
P'Nut, is that you?

P'Apostrophe Nut!
Is that you?
And I finally know
that it is you,
part of the boy who
went away to MMI
to Military School,
the boy who loved
uniforms,
who liked to play
with guns
no matter what I said.

It is the same boy, I guess
I hope.
I pray.
I wait.
God, P'Nut,
I hope it is you.

THE WOMEN'S POEM

The women are wailing,
can you hear?
They are killing our children
in tomato fields
and on battle fields.
Who will save the children from destruction?
Who will save the eyes of our Asian sisters
peering into microscopes of blindness
searching for the light of self-sufficiency
reaping dependency for their toil?

Who will save the children of Namibia
and South Africa
who desire only to breathe the air of freedom
in their own land?
Who will save them from the despots' bullets
and the tyrants' bombs?

The women cry?
Our children are dying
mowed down on the streets
and in our arms,
threatened with death in our bellies.
Our women cry!
Who will birth the generations
if they poison our wombs
in factories, sweat shops
and off shore production?

The women cry!

We are half the world,
we hold up the sky
as hewers of wood,
carriers of water,
reapers of harvest?
Why must we die?
In order to live, to be free?

The women are wailingggggg.
Can you hear?
Who will stand with our men
wrenched from our families in South Africa,
legal slaves sold way from us for bread?
Who will stand with women in the homelands?
What will you do with a million Poppie Nongenas,
sisters in constant struggle,
left without men to the mercy
of Boers and AfriKaners?

Who will save the world from annihilation
by generals in AmeriKA?
Old cowboys in business suits who sit in White Houses
and make wars in other peoples' countries
and send our black, brown, yellow, red,
and white children
to fight over land,
minerals and oil
that belong to other people.

The women cry—Nay,
the women are wailingggggg!
Can you hear them?
Can you hear?

THE HAIR POEM

(For Aikwe)[1]

You know, hair is a political thing.
Like beauty it can make or break you.
If you think this an exaggeration,
try letting your imagination
run home with you for awhile.
Little brown girls in pigtails fret for ribbons and bows
to give the appearance of long even if the hair is short.
Lotta kinky-haired girls
get passed over for promotion,
jobs, gum drops, whistles, and "hey, mamas,"
in favor of curls
even short ones will do as long as they are soft,
bouncing and behaving
as the shampoo people say.
And even in Black Belize City
riding in a taxicab,
the driver says to the braided sister up front
that she need some curls
else she ain't gone never get no husband.
Girlfriend laugh.
We laugh in the back, too.
Two of us dreaded, the other one braided,
we dealing with foo-fool!

When I was little bangs were the thang
and if your mama wouldn't make you some
when you were on chapel program at school,
you were a neglected child.

later on when I got to be a big girl,
being dressed up meant your hair was straightened for sure,
since natural was associated with something
to be kept hidden under a headrag,
to be let out only for taming/straightening
and bringing under control.
The old ladies retaliated by keeping theirs tied up.
I know that now.

All of a sudden—explosion!
Afro became a shout
and afro heads a fact,
black hair began to fly—
uncontrolled—prickly—electric—
questioning, running rampant with the mind inside.
Screaming, affirming, demanding—
invoking fear with the dreaded dread—
the self, the right to be.

A decade passed: All of a sudden—
a bump on the head—
The seventies:
chill—everybody cooled out—wanted to relax—
forget intensity, movement—be American.
Relax.

And pretty soon, black hair relaxed, too
and changed colors—and took on Geri curl,
and tom foolery began with the head again.
And I really do hope
nobody ever makes it easy to change
the style of faces—

Michael Jackson notwithstanding—
because I want to be able
to recognize my kinspeople.

WAKE-UP CALL

Wake up!
Wake up!
This is a wakeup call, y'all
Uh uh. Uh, uh, Uhhhn!
Don't you touch that snooze button!
You ain't got no time for snoozing
while black people still shooting
each other's brains into sidewalks.
You just gone keep on standing round
talking, walking?
Fratricide has replaced genocide
and you still want to hide
underneath the covers
scared to get up, go out,
walk about?
So you keep on snoozing
while we still losing?
This is a wakeup call, y'all.
Open your eyes, look up
stop crying,
We are dying —en masse—
sitting in class
and on the steps with no help

from the leadership.
Wake up!
The ship is sinking,
Scholars thinking
abstract thoughts.
And all for naught.
Nobody left to think about.
Wake up, y'all!

The alarm is ringing
while we are singing
Hip Hop, Rap,
killing is on tap.
You better get the Blues
and don't you push that snooze button
no more to get some more sleep.
Sleep will keep
but death is forever.

L.A. and New York are too close for comfort
Mississippi and Alabama
cannot hide under cover of South.
The world is your oyster!
Open it and find the pearl.
Go into the world.
The phone is ringing.
The alarm is ringing.
Heads are busting,
children are prey
to vultures.
They scream, they cry,
they dream bad dreams of neglect and decay.

Is there no way to bring a new day?
This is A WAKEUP CALL, YALL.
WAKE UP!

---

[1] A twelve-year old who was denied admittance to high school in Belize because he wore dreadlocks

Section 3

Five Decades of Living

Mama's Rubboard Hands

Mama washing
rubboard hands
cold December winter days
with deceptively shiny shining suns
cold to the quick.

Mama washing
rubboard hands
moving endlessly up and down
the tin rubboard
over and over
to clean the clothes held tight
in her rubboard hands
firmly
in the cold or lukewarm water
over and over
up and down
the rubboard
move the rubboard hands
of my mama
cleansing other people's clothes
and souls—
the essence of her being.

Making clean
those rubboard hands
in multiple tasks
diverse usings
the same rubboard hands
stiff fingers

on cold days
hurt fingers that still manage to
caress
to hold in her arms
one child
needing holding . . . I don't remember
being held long,

just long enough
and on the right day
at the right time
those rubboard hands
rubbed my head
plaited my hair
picked at my ears
to see if they were being washed
examined my neck
to make sure it's not getting rusty
from neglect,
looked me over
patted me up

and went on to other washboards at home
underneath the chinaberry tree:
Those washboard, rubboard hands
dished out love
over and over again.

And at night,
those rubboard hands
washed clothes
after seven tin tub baths

starched and ironed white shirts
to boot
with never a cat's face.

Those rubboard hands
pounded out biscuits
myriads of biscuits
in a lifetime
of seven children
and early widowhood.

My Mama's rubboard hands
are magical,
can tease soup from a stone
cook up a stew or pot of greens
that will make you salivate
from the smell alone.
Those rubboard hands
beat cakes out of self-rising flour
and butter
and yard hen's eggs
and was glad to see
Betty Crocker cake mix
which she dutifully beat the 300
strokes it said on the box
with fifty extra for luck thrown in,
in exchange for its predictable sameness.
Our first fast food!

Those rubboard hands picked cotton
and hoed a row,
and planted corn

and sowed ammonium nitrate
around it with her children.

Those rubboard hands were versatile,
sewed many a pinafore dress
out of flour and fertilizer sacks
and from cloth the candy man brought
from faraway places.

Those rubboard hands made
Sunday dresses
with panties to match
and combed many a head of hair
of four girls
especially on Sunday
after church
when widowers came to call,
for dinner and to woo the widow Young.
Those rubboard hands combed hair
until the danger of
any kind of conversation
or proposition(!)
was removed
in front of a child
until the gentleman tire
and take himself home.

Those rubboard hands are awesome.
My Mama is, too.

August 20, 1995

Sharon gone,
Billie Jean,
Mama said on the other end
of the long distance telephone.
Who? Mama,
who you say?
Sharon, little
Sharon, Florene's girl.
Sharon McNeely gone?
Sharon McNeely gone.
Mama cries
I cry
Everybody cries

Five Decades of Living

In five decades of living
I discovered
the Tuskegee Study and
the death of black men
from syphilis and neglect,
and I marveled at integration of schools
and agonize now over what it left.
I discovered genocide,
fratricide, and matricide
in five decades of living.
I learned about school and life

in a course named Living 101
though nobody calls it that.

In five decades of living
I learned that
nothing is ever EXACTLY
the same again.
You can't go back to being innocent
or being a virgin
or being unaware
of hatred, racism or bigotry
in the world.
I was fully 10 years old
before I knew about slavery
and nothing was ever
Exactly the same again.
How can you believe after you find out about
The Middle Passage?
The Holocaust?
Where could you go to find
Innocence again?

In the First Decade
I learned to love,
practiced it on my family,
mourned the death of my father,
and a way of life.
lost trust in adults,
learned to read and write
and love learning.
and 'cipher.

I learned about Friendships,
Widowhood,
And fatherless- ness.
(Especially fatherlessness
after knowing a father.)

I learned the timelessness of ritual in the church—
40 years later, it is the same.

I learned about faith and hypocrisy,
I learned about God,
Jesus, and the prophets,
Egypt and Palestine,
the Virgin Mary and Joseph,
The Three Wise Men,
Abraham and the Ram,
Job and his bedsores,
David and Goliath,
the three Hebrew boys in the fiery furnace
Shadrack, Meshack, and Abednego—
The Creation,
evolution,
school loyalty,
teacher love,
community love,
family love,
Brotherly love,
Sisterly love.
I learned about reaping what you sow,
How to pick cotton, and
Hoe a row,
How to avoid picking cotton

And hoeing a row.

I learned about
Alexander the Great,
and Hannibal.
The Mesopotamia,
and the Nile.

I learned about white folks
and black folks.

In the First Decade,
I learned how to recite
all the books of the Bible,
the states with their capitals first,
my time tables,
the continents of the world.
I imagined them
and prepared for them
although I didn't see them
until the Third.

In the Third Decade
I studied law,
learned analysis,
went through it
and graduated.
And that was the end of that.
I learned that there is no logic in
love for one's brothers and sisters,
friends, or even one's country,
if they don't love you

(and are always stepping on your neck
to boot!)

I learned that Black anger
is very rational, very logical,
and there is no logical way to derive
the love I need to survive
from rationality.
I am logic-challenged,
So I learned to love in AmeriKa
in spite of the right side of my brain.

I learned that Trouble comes
when you least expect it.
That everything can be so right until
you can't even spell wrong
and Trouble will just walk through the door
out of nowhere and get all up in your face.
And no amount of ignoring old Trouble
will make him go away.

I learned that in order to live five decades
I had to learn how to go on living,
forgiving,
when all around me
hatred, bitterness,
and unkind-nessness abound.

I went to the House of Slaves
on Goree Island
in Senegal in 1984
and 10 years later,

to Elmina Castle
on the coast
of Ghana
and learned about
the African slave trade
with the Dutch,
the Portuguese,
and the British.
I learned about Ibrahima,
Prince Among Slaves—
Son of King Siri,
who was enslaved for forty years
in Natchez, Mississippi.
How Ibrahima,
alumnus of Timbuktu,
was always a gentleman,
even in slavery,
during forty years in Natchez.

How Ibrahima,
the Black Moor,
was repatriated to Africa,
and then died,
in the land of his birth.

I learned to forgive the white folks
for slavery
(although after five decades of living,
I do wish the descendants of the slavemasters
would stop trying to absolve themselves
even as they reap its benefits
wearing the knapsack of privilege

about themselves like a halo
the enduring—and rewarding—
legacy of slavery.)

I learned to forgive the Africans
and Mother Africa
for selling off the ancestors
by the shipload,
by the millions.
300 years of it.

I learned to be silent.

I learned the meaning of fear
in the announcement
that the KKK was around the bend
on a Fayetteville road
while marching from Alabama
to Washington, D.C.
to affirm the right to vote.

In the Fourth decade
I learned in Aliceville, Alabama
that you can be scared
and still be moved to action
and that even with tears in my eyes,
I could face police, deputy sheriffs,
standing in my face
with Billy clubs drawn,
and still stand solid on two feet,
singing, in 1982,
"I Shall Not Be Moved!"

for Maggie Bozeman and Julia Wilder
and all the other brave ancestors,
sages, and seers of the past.

And this ain't no play either!

After five decades of living,
your dreams could
shrivel up and die
like a Raisin in the Sun
and people would only feel obligated
to save them
in A Colored Museum
so everybody could laugh
at what ridiculous dreams they are
For Colored Girls Who Have Considered Suicide
When the Rainbow Is Enuf.

After all,
a Day of Absence
does not make one
really white and useful,
it will only advertise your blackness.

I learned second class-ness firsthand
when I realized that the black man
who celebrated fifty years at Judson College
did not include me when he doffed his hat
at girls walking around campus.
It was only when I was walking alone one day
by my black self that he held his head high
looked me straight in the eye

and walked right on by.

I learned that people who just arrived
always assume
you came with them—tedious—
Especially when you feel like asking them
where they've been
all the time you've been there
waiting on them.
But your manners prevail
after five decades
on the planet
and you just smile,
or laughhhhhhhhhhh!
if you simply can't help yourself.

Twenty years later; I still go places
in the world where people of color
look right past me—
while they are shaking my hand—
to the white person next in line.
And did you know that as a black woman
you could be everybody's Mama if you wanted to?
Girls I never knew in college would ease up to me
and ask me questions about sex
or tell me stories about their lives
they couldn't tell anyone else.
And do you know that as a black woman
traveling around the world on airplanes
or whatever,
you will almost never be mistaken
for who you actually are?

I have been mistaken
for a Maid,
for a Caribbean Maid,
an Arkansas Maid
while wearing a blue power suit
and white shirt
in Forrest City,
AND
I have been called
an immigrant maid from anywhere.

Nobody ever mistook me for a college professor
or a lawyer or a poet,
or beachcomber,
or even a beatnik or Grateful Dead,
or nothing like that.

My Africanity is significant
whether or not others choose to accept it.
I wasn't born white
because I was born black—
an African in the Diaspora.
No amount of wishful thinking
underneath
fried or acid conked hair
will change that.
I am who I am.
Self mutilation will not change that.

My Africanity is only one of the things
I refuse to give up—
of my Self, that is.

I learned that there are
some things you can give up:
advice
clothes
love
security
trim...
And even though you might be hard pressed
to do without them,
you could live.
But your Self?
You can't give up your Self
to no Body
or No Thing
'cause who Thing
would want your Self?
But give it away you can
and before you would even know it—
like Poof!
Self out the window—gone!
My name is Black
So to give up my Africanity
is to surrender my name, too,
my whole self.
And I don't like that.

In five decades of living
I learned that you could kill your fool self working—
if you don't watch out.
And there will be nobody around to say:
"Watch out, don't do that!"
Not your lover

nor your brother
nor your sister
not your mother
not your husband
No MAN or WO-man.
You could die.
You could die waiting on somebody
to tell you to stop working your fool self to death.

Lonne Elder said it best in "Ceremonies in Dark Old Men,"
when Odessa says:
"Who the hell ever told a black woman
she was some kinda savior?"

I say: Why did she believe it?

You don't have to be the strongest,
the bravest, nor the least afraid.
You could be an ordinary colored girl
and still love yourself.
And if you love your pretty black self
nobody else can help themselves
from doing the same thing!

In five decades of living
I discovered
what it means
to be Somebody
in some time
and some place.
Later on,

I discovered what it means
to be nobody.

In five decades of living I learned
that by the time your children learn how to appreciate you,
  you are nearly always too old to appreciate them!
Somebody ought to tell children early on
that every child who ever lived
thought s/he was smarter than the parents who nourished her.
And most every child was wrong, too!

In five decades of living I learned that
if there were some way to pass on knowledge to others
by those who have gone this way before,
the drama of life would be no less riveting.
Every generation chooses to walk the same path,
make the same mistakes and learn its own lessons
in its own way.
The learning is no less the stuff of novels—
in spite of the sameness of the ritual—
new and diversified for the un-lived children.
So they wade through the same
muck and mire
as their ancestors,
always thinking that they are
wading in new waters,
breaking New Ground,
riding new waves.
In reality, they only walk among
new names.
They tread upon the same
old streets and alleys,

ride the same waves,
and wait out the same hurricanes
as their parents did.

There is nothing new about it.

The outrageous clothes,
The outrageous hair,
The outrageous lifestyles,
The Foolishness.
The Drinking.
The Wild Dancing.
The Drugs.
The Sleeping Around.
The Shacking.
The Abortions.
The Music.
All have the ring of new—newly named.

But new it is not:

It is only the old recycled lives
of our parents and grandparents
that we live,
cycling and peddling the abuse
of ourselves
from generation to generation,
family to family,
culture to culture.

People don't change all that much.

In five decades of living
I discovered
that lonely the world over spells
L-O-N-E-L-Y
and that there is no mistaking it
for what it is.
I discovered that loneliness
feels the same
in any language
or culture
you care to speak
or live it in.

It can be Christmas lonely
or New Year's lonely
or Love lonely,
or Holiday lonely,
or Everyday lonely.
All feels the same—Lonely.

In five decades of living,
I learned that a Black woman,
has No Place to be Somebody,
and that Dark Old Men living in
Ceremonies really have nowhere else to go.

I learned that The Amen Corner
is where people go to
when the ancient need
for reconciliation
is upon them.
God has already shown them

that they are mortal and
they have been perfectly cowed.

I learned that even the church can fail you—
Man Kind in the church—that is.

I learned that to bare one's soul
is to risk ridicule, scorn and contempt
from those who would deny you
your nervous breakdown.

Those who know me will only occasionally
be fascinated by me
and not disappointed
the way friends tend to be.

I learned to take my worst self last
amongst those who know me best.

And I learned over time
that you can
learn and learn and learn,
time after time—
overtime!—
and never fully learn a thing.

In five decades of living,
I discovered that you must make your own way
if you want to walk the walk.
You must clear a path,
set a sail,
open a hatch,

and walk through it,
or crawl if you have to,
and make your own way
for yourself.
Nobody can do it for you.
Terrie Wilson says it well:
"You have to buy your own sailboat if you want to sail!
Nobody is going to let you sail his sailboat
the way you want to sail.
You've got to have your own sailboat if you want to sail."

After five decades of living I learned
when you heal yourself,
you have to walk
backwards to wellness
through the various stages
of your getting sick—
painful as it is—
in order to go forward,
in order to heal yourself

A few things I learned from scratch
about depression
and being down in the dumps:
Do not expect others to listen to you.
Be glad if they do.
(People rarely listen to themselves.
If they did, do you think people would say
the things they say to you?)

In five decades of living
I learned that people rarely

hide themselves from you
and when they manage to do it,
it is only because they didn't know
who they were in the first place.

Yes, people always tell you who they are.
No matter what they say or do
how they re-present
and present
themselves—
they will—
always tell you who they are.
And if you aren't careful,
you won't hear it,
or listen to it.
Or you will dismiss it
if you don't know
what you're hearing
when it is said.

In five decades of living,
I learned that one friend
connected to you by affinity
rather than blood,
is worth a thousand family
not so connected.
Treat your friends well;
they are your adult family
once you leave the nest.
Do not take
your youthful friendships lightly.
Cherish them tenderly instead.

They are the basis of your life,
the underpinnings of your confidence,
your trust in the world.
There will never be another time—
save war and foxholes or such stresses
you would just as soon avoid—
when you will bond so completely
with another as in your youth.
Savor it. Hold friendship dear.
You will never be able
to trust so completely again—
no matter how hard you try—
as in the innocence of youth.

After five decades of living
I still have trouble
accepting
that all is lost
that peace can't be regained
that right can't be policy
that children are grownups
that grownups are children
that George Wallace loves me—
like fob he does!
I still go places in the world
where people ask me why
black people put George Wallace
back in office.
Why?
Like why do children lie?
Why do adults pretend to speak the truth?
Why do in-laws assume you don't like them?

Why?
Why do churches full
of otherwise intelligent people
pay preachers to shout at them
about nothing that changes their sorry state
every Sunday morning?
Why?
Why do people live and die
wrapped up in lies
afraid to speak truth
even to themselves?
Why?
Why?
Why?

In five decades of living,
I learned to say:
Stop it!
I am not the last Black woman you knew
Stop it!
Nor am I the Black woman you just compared me to.
Stop it!
I am who I am.
I am. I am.
Rural woman,
Salty, unafraid
Not politically correct,
nor looking for the right thing to say.

In five decades of living,
I learned to cherish myself,
the blemishes

and imperfections of tone,
size, shape or appointment.

I learned to embrace the old—
to put it with fine things like
wine,
lace,
memories,
emotions.
To cherish the evolution
into an almost whole person.

AND I DON'T QUITE KNOW
WHERE I'M GOING NEXT.

Tomorrow Comes

Dear Kathy,

Tomorrow comes.

Count your blessings, we are told.
Children in Africa are starving,
and the TV regularly shows
those washed up by typhoons in Bangladesh.
Count your blessings we are told.
Your ancestors of old
were slaves and worked themselves to death
instead of starving
or washing out to sea.

Count your blessings.
Little children say your prayers
don't despair
life can repair
any damage already done.
God can heal
even old wounds
if you allow the God in you to shine through
and heal yourself.
What do they tell children in Africa and Bangladesh?

The thunder roars in Alabama.
Rains come
and wash away my tracks
cut off my shadow
strike the inane telly
and the chattering answer machine
but not me.
And I don't know
if yesterday will ever repeat itself
but tomorrow comes
in the morning—fresh
sometimes with rain
sometimes old Sol
mercilessly beating down
on bare heads.
But surely tomorrow comes,
and there are no re-runs.

January in the South

Dear Kathy,

It's January.
Even in Alabama,
the weather is inclement,
unruly,
unkind, not clement.
I struggle to keep warm,
to find peace in January
and solace in the certainty
of Spring coming
'round the calendar
when she comes.

It's January and people die
and are buried.
Funerals are held
and old hurts and wounds
are exposed:
Who is a Child
and who is ill-begotten,
illegitimate,
outside Child,
or Child-nobody-knew-about
or Child Denied.
People raising Cain,
accusing,
abusing,
bringing up all kinds of old hurts
and pains,

and slights,
and everything.
The scabs come off,
old wounds bleed,
and new people know
old truths
that hurt just like before,
until the scab covers it over again.

To hibernate in winter is easier
if you are used to sleeping anyway.
Sleeping is healing.
Somnolence is avoidance
of cold and usurping weather outside-
an insult to the bones
and joints.
Hibernation is a lot easier
if you have nothing to walk about for,
nothing to say,
or just prefer to hide anyway.

Where will I hibernate when I am moved to speak?
Will the planet miss me if I'm gone?
Will the planet even know that I was here?
Who will tell the stories if not I?

Muriel Rukeyser said:

If just one woman stood up
and told the truth about her life
the world would split wide open.

Can I get a witness?

What do you see when you look at me?

Nappy Head
and linty dread,
sassafras and
sage,
Lapa and cufi
and tie dye
and loud, loud
print,
and strong body,
and descriptive speech,
and wayward feet,
and miles and miles
of walking. WALKING

Behind a slave coffle
from North Carolina to Alabama—WALKING
dragging a cotton sack
up and down a plantation row—
or walking the woods to school.
These feet are tired of walking
but they walk on.
One day they will stop.
They will stand still,
while I stand up and tell the truth
about my life.

Two Women Talking
about what?

What we have learned,
seen, and heard.
What we know.

Marge Tuitte was a great big
ship of a woman
in the US of A
Arah Hector stood tall
in Antigua.
Jackie Creft was fearlessly
forging a new way with Maurice Bishop
in Grenada.
Regina was a wild woman in the whirlwind
in Belize.

Sisters all.
They stood tall
and told big truths
to set the world straight,
loudly, boldly,
going up against Goliath
speaking to power
with the might of truth
on their side.

They all crossed over to the other side. Finis?

Who will acknowledge that they were here, if not I?
Who will avenge their passing?
Who will finish their story?
(Other people will tell your story
and it is not your story anymore.

It is their story, His-Story.)

Where is Herstory?

Where will the children learn the truth
if not from our lives?
Let it ring. Let the truth ring!
Our children will live lies
if we tell not the truth,
if we hide the truth
if Herstory is not written down.

Fannie Lou walked
the walk
and talked the talk.
Who but me to tell her story?

Did your grandmother talk to you?

I wish mine had.
Some days I tell my Mama stories
about other people
when we are alone
and I don't leave out the risque parts.
At first, she blushes
and then we laugh,
big, out loud,
marveling in our recklessness,
stretching the gut,
good, strong, belly laughs.

I take my laughs where I can find them.

There is so little to laugh about in the world.

I wish I had all the stories written down
so I could read them
so I could pass them on
so I could be sure nobody would alter them.
Then I could be sure that our children
and their children,
and everybody's children to come
could
read them
and know
that we passed this way once,
and maybe, just maybe,
there won't be a need
to retrace these steps again.

Mama used to say:
If you step in your tracks
on the way back home,
you will get a headache.
Well
If you walk the same road,
cover the same tracks,
mistakes and all,
you will get the same headaches
as when you first walked it madly.

Stand still.

We can stand up and tell the truth about our lives.

It's January in the South, too.
I love you.

Fear Not The Fall

Fear not the fall.
Better to fall from the strength
of the sound of one's voice
speaking truth to the people
than to spend a lifetime
mired in discontent,
groveling in the sty of certainty
of acceptance,
of pseudo-love,
of muteness,
and easy-to-be-around-ness.

Better to fall screaming—
arms flailing,
legs askew
clawing in your intensity
for the right to be—
than silently,
like a weakened snowbird,
sentenced to the boredom of earth
too sick to sing.

Fannie Lou Hamer: This Little Light . . .

≫ A Two-Act Drama ≪

ACT I

FANNIE LOU HAMER: (*Sings*)

Pee-pi, pee-pi, where you little lamb?
Way down in the valley.
Birds and the butterflies picking at his eyes
and the po' lil' thing it cry, mama.
Mama gone, papa gone,
they shall bring some horses,
white and black, purple and gray,
all them pretty little horses.
When you wake, you'll eat a hoecake
and ride the pretty little pony.
Go to sleep, go to sleep, go to sleepy little baby.
Mama run away, papa couldn't stay,
there's nobody but the baby.
Go to sleep, with your by you ba,
go the sleepy little baby.

I ain't no stranger to struggle. My mama taught me that
song; her mama taught it to her. My granmama was a slave. I
used to sing that song to my babies, too. See, we had to leave
the babies on the end of the row while we was picking cotton,
and you would just have to hope and pray that the antses and
flies and mosquitoes and things didn't get on your baby. Every
year, we get through picking cotton, sheer-cropping for the

white man, my mama still wouldn't have no money to feed us, so she would ask the people for the little cotton they had done left in the field, and didn't want to be bothered with trying to gather, if we could scrap it. We would just walk for miles and miles, sometimes it would be cold and the ground would be frozen over and we wouldn't have no shoes, and my mama would take paper and rags and tie our feet up. And we would just walk from field to field picking cotton, my mama and her chillun, scrapping cotton.

(*Sings*)

> Pee-pi, pee-pi, where you little lamb?
> Way down in the valley.
> Birds and the butterflies picking at his eyes
> and the po' lil' thing it cry, mama.
> Mama gone, papa gone,
> they shall bring some horses,
> white and black, purple and gray,
> all them pretty little horses.

ISSAQUENA: That was Mrs. Fannie Lou Hamer, or at least that's how I saw her one day talking to a bunch of small children over in Edwards, Mississippi. "Every once in a now and then somebody moves in such a way that makes us jerk up and take notice. Mrs. Hamer made some decisions during the 1960s that made some of us stand up and follow; feeling a little stronger and going a little further because of the chances she took—Mississippi will never be the same!" Bernice Reagon said that about Mrs. Fannie Lou Hamer. Miss Hamer made me jerk up and take notice. I'm Issaquena Hopewell and I'm still hopeful that something good can come of me. I'm still hopeful that something good can come of you, too. That's why I wanna tell you about this woman, name of Fannie Lou . . . Hamer was her name. I love my Southland, I like the soil and yes, I like the dirt, and yes, I picked a little cotton, too. "Jump down turn around, pick a bale of cotton, jump down turn around, pick a bale a day . . ." When she was six years old, Miss Hamer got tricked into picking cotton. Before that she was a little child playing on the end of the row. See, children during those days didn't get hold of fruit and junk food like they do now everytime somebody comes from the store. My mama says at Christmas time, (and she right along the same age with Miss Hamer) they would get an apple and an orange and maybe a little stick of peppermint candy if they were lucky. And the rest of the time, you didn't see no treats. You remember how loud apples and oranges used to smell at Christmas time? That's cause it was an unfamiliar smell to you. Those smells didn't enter the house too often. Anyway, the man told Fannie Lou that if she picked thirty pounds of cotton that day, she could have anything she wanted from the commissary. That was his store, on the plantation. Fannie Lou was just a baby girl, and you know she wanted those treats out of the store. So she picked cotton hard, this little crippled girl trying to pick thirty pounds of cotton (you know she had polio when she was a child). Course, the plantation owner was delighted when she did. He just rared back and laughed and gave her a cookie and some gum that she picked out at the store. And the next day, you see, he required her to pick sixty pounds. That's how Fannie Lou started on her cotton picking career at age six. When she quit picking cotton thirty-nine years later, she was forty-five years old and she was picking two hundred to three hundred pounds of cotton a day.

This sharecropping thing was a evil system that replaced

slavery. Some people called it working on halves, all about the same—slavery, sharecropping, or on halves—you do the work, white man get the money. Didn't make no difference what you called it. Come to think of it, Miss Hamer was good at looking at things with a straight eye, and calling it what it was. She was a direct person, wasn't after no foolishness and beating around the bush—and she would tell you how she felt about things, not just tell you something to make you think she agrees with you like some people do. I saw her at one of those women's conventions that was so popular many years ago in the East one time, Miss Hamer had been invited to speak. Well, you know, the woman who spoke before Miss Hamer really let the hammer down. Women had just started to talking out loud about how low down some men could be. So, this woman went on and on, and on about how bad all the men were. Miss Hamer was the next speaker.

FANNIE LOU: I don't know 'bout y'all's mens, but my man is a tall man, and we both know how to stand up!

ISSAQUENA: She was through with that. Mrs. Hamer had a way of getting right to the point of things. Now, Miss Hamer was talking about her husband, Perry Hamer. People call him Pap. Good man. Miss Hamer was a good woman. She and Pap was good for each other. Miss Hamer and Pap would come in from the field some time and when they was through with supper and everything, they would sit out on the porch and talk, try to cool off before they went to bed.

FANNIE LOU: Come on, give mama some sugar fore you go to bed; that's it, give Pap some sugar, too. Now say your prayers, God gone know if you don't say your prayers. Now, git, git to bed. Good nite. You know school done started. Pity and a shame ain't nothing up there at that raggedy school but the teachers and them walls and the chillun. Chillun is apt, too. You know them chillun what come in here from up north, them is apt chillun, too. You know they tell me that Negroes can vote in other places; that we is got a right to vote. Naw, like in the 'lections. You know, like they have in Sunflower County, like to vote for school board, sheriffs and things. You hear 'em talking 'bout it all the time, who winning and everything, but you don't hear 'em say nothing 'bout us voting. Well, if colored peoples is voting in other places, then we oughta be 'lowed to vote heah. What 'cha think? Make any kinda sense to you? Pap, I wanna go to Indianola to try to register to vote. Well, yes, I know we got to eat and sleep, but that's all we ever been working for, Pap, eating and sleeping. We ain't got nothing but ourself and these chillun, and a new debt every yeah. I know we could do better than this. Pap, don't you see? This 1962; I'm forty-five years old. We not getting no younger. We running this place. I'm the timekeeper here. I know what this place make; you do, too, 'cause you managing it. Aw, they ain't gone never call you the manager but you doing it just the same. But it ain't gone never do nothing for us. I'm thinking 'bout the chirren and you and me, too. Aw, Pap, I done already signed my name to the list to go to Indianola to register next Friday. Don't you think one of us should go? Nothing fail but a try and we sho ain't got nothing to lose. Pap? Pap?

(*Sings*)
Cum bah yeah, my Lawd, cum bah yeah;
Cum bah yeah, my Lawd, cum bah yeah;
Cum bah yeah, my Lawd, cum bah yeah;
O' Lawd, cum bah yeah.

FANNIE LOU: Our Heavenly Father, I come before your throne of undeserved kindness with bowed head and humbled heart. Asking you to show me the way, Lord. We lost chillun crying in the wilderness on these plantations in Mississippi, and we need you to guide us and protect us, and teach us what is right. Jesus, it was you who said that out of the mouths of babies the truth should come. If these chillun is telling us the right thing Lord, if there is a way to change Mississippi to make things better for colored people, show us now. If this is what you set before me, Lord, then I don't want nothing else. If it's your will for me to be a slave, show me, Lord. But if this not your will, show me what to do. Lord, you said if we take one step, you'll take two; I want you to hear me now. I come before you in the name of Jesus, Lord. Show us what to do. Help us, teach us, guide us, go with these young folks, go with all of us, the old folks and the young folks, help us to see the truth. And Lord if it's not in your will, I don't want no parts of it, but if it's your will, Lord, if you want us to make a move, Jesus, I beg you, just show me some kind of sign. If you help us, Lord, I promise to obey you and do your will, I promise to go in your name, Lord, show us the shining star, lead us out of the darkness in Mississippi, we want you to go with us, stand by us. We know that we are your chillun, that you is a powerful God. And I know, Father, that with you all things is possible. You can deliver us from the hand of iniquity and from the jaw of the lion just like you delivered Jonah from the belly of the whale, just like you was with the Hebrew boys in the fiery furnace, went down with Moses to Egypt and told old Pharoh to let your people go, I know, Lord, that you can deliver us. This is your humble servant, Lord, Fannie Lou, asking you, Jesus, to innercede for the dark chillun of Mississippi. We your chillun, Lord, you said so, we know, Lord that you don't make no difference in respect of color. Well, your chillun is suffering Lord, in Mississippi, and I'm coming to you in the only way I know how, on my knees, begging you Jesus, to have mercy, have mercy on us, O Lord. Have mercy upon your lost chillun. And when all is said and done, done all we can do on this earth, and the old flesh is dead and rotten, I ask for a home in your kingdom, Father. Yes! Yes! In Jesus name we pray, Amen.

(Sings)

Ask the Savior to help you,
Comfort, strengthen and keep you,

Jesus is willing to help you,
He will carry you through.

FANNIE LOU: Well you know, today's the day, Pap, for me to go to Indianola to put my name on the voters registration list. Now, Pap, what kinda answer is that. "If I got to go, I got to go?" I would have a fit if I turn over one morning and I didn't find you in the bed. But I got to go. I got to. OK? OK.

That's what he meant. "If I got to go, I got to go." Pap understand; Pap a mess. Know what he told me 'bout going down here to register? "Fannie Lou, ya picking in the right cotton to get your hundred." Huh!

"Good Morning, my name is Fannie Lou Hamer and I'm here to register to vote." (*She practices saying it*) "My name is Fannie Lou Hamer and I'm here to register to vote. Yes'm, Fannie Lou, that's my name, yes'm, register to vote. Probably be more like that!

(Sings)

Ain't gonna let nobody turn me 'round,
Turn me round, turn me 'round;
Ain't gonna let nobody turn me 'round,
Gonna keep on a walking, keep on a talking,
Marching up the freedom lane.
Ain't gonna let no police turn me 'round,
Turn me 'round, turn me 'round,
Ain't gonna let no police turn me 'round,
I'm gonna keep on walking, keep on talking,
Marching up the freedom lane.

ISSAQUENA: Now, the white people was mad about these eigh-
teen colored people going to Indianola on a bus to try to
register to vote. They even called Fannie Lou's boss man, old
man Cropper. Now Cropper was really mad: Here was Fannie
Lou right up under his nose, pulling something like that. So
when the courthouse people called him to let him know that
one of the colored people off his place was in Indianola trying
to vote, he went straight to Pap. Thought Pap didn't know
nothing 'bout it. "Well, Pap, do you know what Fannie Lou is
doing?" Pulling his hands in and out of his khaki pants pocket,
and he was already sweating that early, so his shirt and his hair
was plastered to his head. He was hot! "Pap, do you know what
that woman is doing, your wife?" Pap stood back and looked at
him: "Yes, sir, my wife told me where she was going when she
left home." Well, that was kind of a surprise to old man
Cropper, got really red in the face when Pap said that. "Well,
you tell Fannie Lou I wanna see her soon as she get home." And
he went back across the road to his own house. Well, soon as
Miss Hamer come home, Cropper was back out in the yard
wanting to talk to her. "Fannie Lou, I like you and Pap, y'all
hard-working people, earnest people, like to keep y'all 'round.

But I can't have you down at that courthouse stirring up trouble. You gon' have to go down there and take your name off that vote list, or get offa my place one." Miss Hamer was ready for that: "Well, no sir, I was registering for myself; I didn't register for you." Well, the upshot of that was Cropper put Miss Hamer out that night. Her and the children, Virgie Ree, and Dorothy, went and stayed with the deacon's wife that night. Pap took 'em and he come on back home. Next morning, here come Cropper again. "Well, Pap, what did Fannie Lou say?" You know a white person can ask you a impossible question, "What you think my wife say when you put her out of her house, white man?" Pap was saying to hisself.

Pap looked at 'im. "Well you know she gone cause you told her she couldn't stay here. I'm gone finish my crop and I'm gone be gone." Cropper knowed he was beat then. He jumped back. Had finally hit that white man in his hip pocket where it hurt! "You tell Fannie Lou to come on back home, then, things'll be just like they always was." This time, Pap put his hands in his overall bib, pulled on the straps and popped the strap. "Well, no sir, she say that's just the trouble, she don't want things to be like they always was!" Pap took Miss Hamer and the children to a little house in the woods and they stayed there till he finished the crop and got them a house in Ruleville off the plantation.

Now, Miss Hamer'nem name was mud. People say they was running like rats! Put out their house. You know how people do. Look around Miss Hamer would be gone all the time. People say she was with the civil rights workers. Something was going on all the time. Sometimes Miss Hamer would take other people to meetings with her. It was mostly SNCC students and workers here (this is SNCC country); SCLC mostly had a lot of workshops and training in other states. Miss

Hamer was coming from a workshop with some more people when she was put in jail in Winona, Mississippi. See, they were "sitting in" at the lunch counters in those little high-priced coffee shops they have in the bus stations. Well, that worked for a while but when they got to Winona, Mississippi, they were arrested. You ever see somebody get a whipping? See it was mostly ladies/women. Miss Hamer, June Johnson, Euvester Simpson, Miss Annelle Ponder, and James West. They carted those people off to jail. Now I didn't see it, but they tell me those people took a beating. Say the white people beat them to within a inch of their lives. Had prisoners whipping Miss Hamer. Black people. Don't that make you mad? Wa-show! Wa-show!

FANNIE LOU: Well, Pap, I was PICKING IN THE RIGHT COTTON FIELD TO GET MY HUNDRED. Hell, Baby, I picked a whole bale. No, it's all right. I want to sit up, I can sit up, I need to talk to you, Pap, and tell you how I feel. Naw, not this, these just old fleshy wounds, they'll heal up. I need to tell you what happened to me inside, being in jail, getting beat up, listening to them innocent chillun crying and screaming. It done something to me, Pap. I ain't scared. Oh, I can't say I wasn't scared while it was happening. We was all scared. I was so scared for them chillun I had wit me, scared one of 'em might get killed and it would be on my conscience that I led 'em to they death. I didn't want to have to face they parents about that. But God is good, and He let us all live.

They tried to kill us, Pap. When they come at me, they had a big colored man, a prisoner, and he beat me for them while they stood around and looked, drinking. And they give him whiskey and he beat me until my skin was hard, baby, and all the time they was callin me a communist or something, making out like I done something to hurt somebody, asking me questions about other people. And when that prisoner got tired, they brought out another colored prisoner and he beat me some more. They beat us until they couldn't have no fun out of it no more. And I kept hearing them talking. They was lower than dogs, Pap. They tried to fool us out the jail one nite so they could shoot us down and say we was trying to escape. I wont scared no more, and I told them you just gone haveta kill me in my cell, I ain't going nowhere. Euvester Simpson was in the cell with me. They didn't know what to do with us, Pap. I could hear 'em talking about putting us in the river and you know, it's a funny thing Pap, the more scared they got about what they had done, the braver I felt. I wasn't scared no more. It didn't make no difference whether they beat me any more or not. I wasn't scared. Thought maybe I was going crazy for not being scared. Shh, don't say it. I can't hate nobody. I feel sorry for them jailers and sheriffs; I feel sorry for anybody that could let hate wrap them up; ain't no such a thing as I can hate anybody and hope to see God's face, no matter how evil they is. Shh, shh, Pap. I know. Don't say it. You know I'm gon' be right back out there for us. We can make it, just don't let nothing separate us. It's you and me, Pap, forever.

(*Sings*)

Gonna lay down my burdens down by the riverside,
Down by the riverside, down by the riverside
Gonna lay down my burdens down by the riverside,
To study war no more. I ain't gone study war no more,
I ain't gone study war no more, I ain't gone study war no more.

ACT II

FANNIE LOU: (*Mass meeting speech*) From the fourth chapter of St. Luke, beginning at the eighteenth verse: "The spirit of the Lord is upon me, because he has *annointed* me to *preach* the *gospel* to the poor ... He have sent me to bind up the brokenhearted, *preach deliverance* to the captives, and *recovery of sight* to the blind, to set at *liberty them that are bound, to preach the acceptable year of our Lord.*" Now, the time has come that was Christ's purpose on earth. And we've only been getting by by paying our way to hell. But the time is out. While Simon of Serene was helping Christ to bear his cross up the hill, he said, "Must Jesus bear this cross alone and all the world go free?" He said, "No, there's a cross for everyone, and there's a cross for me. This consecrated cross I'll bear 'til death shall set me free. And then go home a crown to wear, for there's a crown for me."

And there's no easy way out; we've just got to wake up and face it, folks. And if I can face the issue, you can, too. You see, things what's so pitiful about it, the men been wanting to be the boss all these years, and the ones that ain't up under the house is under the bed. But you see, that's poison, it's poison for us not to speak for what we know is right. As Christ said from the seventeenth chapter of Acts and the twenty-sixth verse: "Hadth made of one blood all nations for to dwell on the face of the earth." Then, it's no difference to have different colors. And, brother, you can believe this or not; I've been sick of this system for as long as I can remember.

I heard some people speak of depression in the Thirties. In the Sixties it was 'pression with me. Depression! I haven't been as hungry, it's a funny thing, since I started working for Christ. It's kinda like in the 23rd Psalm when He said: "Thou prepareth a table before me in the presence of mine enemy. Thou anointed my head with oil and my cup runneth over." And I have walked through the valley and the shadow of death, because it was on the 10th of September in 1962 when they shot sixteen times in a house. And there it wont a foot over the bed where my head was, but that night I wont there. Don't you see what God can do? Quit running around trying to dodge them, because this Book say, "He that seeketh to save his life shall lose it anyhow." So, as long as you know you're going for something, you put up the life. Then we can be like Paul say: "I have fought a good fight, and I have kept the faith." You know, it's been a long time. People, I have worked, I have worked hard as anybody. I have been picking cotton and would be so hungry, and one of the poison things about it, would be wondering what I was gone cook that night. But, you see, all of them things was wrong, see. And I have asked God, and I've said, "My Lawd . . . (and you have, too, and there ain't no need in you lying and saying you ain't!) My Lawd, please to open the way for us, to please make a way for us where I can stand up and speak for my race and speak for these hungry children." And he opened the way and all of them opened a bank account. You, see, he made it so plain for us. He sent a man to Mississippi, was the same man Moses had with him to go to Egypt, tole him to go down in Miss'ippi and tell Ross Barnett to let my people go!

(*Sings*)

This little light of mine, I'm gone let it shine,
This little light of mine, I'm gone let it shine,
This little light of mine, I'm gone let it shine,
Let it shine, let it shine, let it shine.
Everywhere I go, I'm gone let it shine,
Everywhere I go, I'm gone let it shine,
Everywhere I go, I'm gone let it shine,
Let it shine, let it shine, let it shine.
This little light of mine, I'm gone let it shine,
This little light of mine, I'm gone let it shine,
This little light of mine, I'm gone let it shine,
Let it shine, let it shine, let it shine.

ISSAQUENA: Well, rocked on, rocked on. It was a lot of people getting registered to vote in the state of Mississippi. Black people, poor people, black and white, but they ran up against a problem. The regular Democratic Party in Mississippi wouldn't let the people participate as Democrats with them. In 1964, coming upon the presidential elections, the people decided to organize a party of their own, a political party of their own. Miss Hamer 'nem organized the Mississippi Freedom Democrats, held an election statewide in Mississippi and took sixty-eight delegates to the Democratic National Convention in Atlantic City, New Jersey, and asked the national Democrats to seat them instead of the all-white regular Democratic Party delegation. Miss Hamer 'nem got dressed up; they even had a chance to sit in smoke-filled rooms.

FANNIE LOU: Senator Humphrey, I ain't no stranger to struggle. You know, lots of things happen to you in this Movement work. But I been in a struggle all my life, Senator Humphrey. It was a struggle to get sixty-eight of us here as delegates from the cotton fields of Mississippi to Atlantic City, New Jersey, to the National Democrat convention, but we kept a-struggling and we made it here. And we is asking you to help. Now, we organized this Mississippi Freedom Democratic Party because of a struggle. I'm the Vice President and I'm representing the Freedom Democrats here today because the President of the MFDP is in jail this minute in Mississippi because of a struggle for freedom. We are struggling in Mississippi as colored people who is being denied the right to vote. We knows that. I don't wanna know about the Democratic Party and the Vice Presidential nomination. It's the reg'lar Democrats that's fighting us in Miss'ippi. Senator Humphrey, you can help us in this struggle if you want to; you just got to get up your nerve and go in there and do it!

Mr. Wilkins, I know that you is a good spokesperson for the Negro peoples, and for the NAACP. I'm is not a sophisticated a politician as you. And I know that you can speak clearer than me . . . sometimes. But, you know, Mr. Wilkins, I ain't never seed you in my community in Miss'ippi, and them is the people I represents, them is the people I speak for. And they done already told me that we didn't come all this-a way for no two seats, since all-a us is tired!

Senator Humphrey, I know lots of people in Miss'ippi who have lost they jobs for trying to register to vote. I had to leave the plantation where I lived and worked in Sunflower County. Now, if you lose this job of Vice President because you help the MFDP, everything will be all right, God will take care of you. But if you take this Vice President nomination like this, why, you will never be able to do any good for civil rights, poor people, for peace, or any of them things you talk about.

Senator Humphrey, I'm gone pray to Jesus for you.

Mr. Chairman, and the Credentials Committee, my name is Mrs. Fannie Lou Hamer and I live at 626 East Lafayette Street, Ruleville, Sunflower County, Mississippi. It was the 31st of August, 1962, that eighteen of us traveled to Indianola to try to become first-class citizens. We was met by Mississippi mens, highway patrolmens, and they only allow two of us to take the literacy test at a time. We were not allowed to register to vote in the state of Mississippi. And I was run away from my home the same day because I refused to take my name off the application. And we have been fighting for our lives ever since. In 1963, six of us was taken off a bus in Winona, Mississippi, and carried to jail and beat to within a inch of our lives. I was placed in a cell with a young woman called Miss Euvester Simpson. I begin soon to hear sounds of licks and horrible screams. "Can you say, yes sir, Nigger! Can you say yes sir?!" And I could hear Annelle Ponder screaming, then I hear her praying; and it wasn't too long before three white mens come to my cell for me.

ISSAQUENA: Now when Miss Hamer started to telling 'bout the beating, President Johnson called a press conference, some of 'em say it was because they spotted an iceberg over in East Siberia. Some say it was to get Miss Hamer off the TV. Now, you see the President got Miss Hamer off the TV then, but Miss Hamer was the kind of woman you couldn't shut her mouth. She continued over the years and as the Movement grew, Miss Hamer did too. She gave interviews to people sometimes in the years to follow. And after that, she just spoke for herself!

FANNIE LOU: I thank you; I thank you. To the president of

Morehouse College, faculty and student body, brothers and sisters: I want to thank you for inviting me here. I have just left Tougaloo College where this morning I received a honorary Doctorate of Humane Letters; and I am on my way to Howard University where I expect to receive another honorary Doctorate of Humane Letters. And I wants to thank you, Morehouse, for this Plaque.

FANNIE LOU: Sunflower County, I think, is worse than Rhodesia, South Africa, because it is Smith with a power structure over there, and it's one man here, the Senator, and these landowners is the worst in the world. They are beginning to tell the people that they shouldn't get registered, and telling 'em to leave the freedom schools alone. And they using these poverty programs for one of the biggest political frauds in the history of our time and they are using our kids like political football. And we are fighting this because it's so unjust. The director of the CAP agency admitted to me that the chairman of the poverty program in Sunflower County is a member of the White Citizen Council. Still, the government grant people like that money to enslave us more. We need federal registrars to get the people registered in Sunflower County, and some political education so that they will understand this white man's trick because as long as this white man control the money, he's gone control the Negro. We need us some land so we don't have to be dependent on this man; got to get us a freedom farm. Now we have proof that they going to people that's been on welfare and telling 'em if they didn't get their children away from those freedom schools where we been set up, you know, some people teaching a year, some nine months out of the year, that they wasn't gone get any welfare 'til they pull 'em out the freedom schools and put them in the white. It's the biggest, it's the biggedest, crookedest stuff that ever was handed out through Washington, D.C., and 'tis nothing but political tricks.

Sunflower County is still one of the most poverty-stricken places in the whole country. People for the past, I say three hundred years, been eating poke and grits—poking they feet under the table and gritting they teeth. And we just about tired of that, too.

You see, the thing about these bills, it's okay to pass a bill, but what are you gone do about enforcing the laws already on the books. If the Constitution means something to me, enforce it. Lot of people think because we had a Voting Right Bill, everything is all right. But it's not. They do a lot of things undercover, but they do the same thing. If they get a chance, they'll lynch a man just as quick as they did in 1925. They is working to preserve segregation and one way they can do it is to use this poverty money to get a whole lot of work done on these plantations so they can keep they money and use it to keep things more segregated than they was. You see, this white man know how to faneuver; we got to learn how to faneuver, too. You know, this here poverty money is just like manna. We can stand here and catch it when they drop it outta Washington, D.C., but if we don't learn how to make us none, we ain't gone never have none. That's economic power. It disturbs me very much that for four hundred years, whites identified with white power, and one innocent man said, black power, and look like it's gone turn the world upside down. You know, you have Jewish Holidays, the Italians have a holiday, white people have their day, Puerto Ricans, St. Patrick Day, but black people can't say a thing. This is a tactic. We just got to understand that ever' nation on earth got to identify with its people, wherever they are. It's nothing wrong with being black and if we get any power whatsoever, what would you call it?

You couldn't say pink power, it's black power, but the press is treating us like criminals. They even tried to brand me a communist and I know as much 'bout communism as a horse do about Christmas. Do communism mean the same thing as the things we fighting for? I've never seen a communist to know one in my life. Communism? We fighting hungryism, the right to eat, have a decent job, a home. A lot of people can't understand what I mean when I say I'm not fighting for equal rights. If you raise questions about all the things we've been faced with in this country and we have been the only people in this country that've been nonviolent and could stand up for dignity and human respect, you can understand what I mean when I say I'm not fighting for equal rights. You think about the background of a white man what they have done to the Indians and what they have done to every generation after generation of human beings you can understand why I don't want equal rights. I'm fighting for something they never knowed too much about, human rights. See, whether you Jewish, Chinese, Mexican, Indian, Italian, Japanese, Puerto Rican, whatever race you are, I'm concerned about you if you a human being. And they don't know too much about human respect 'cause if they did, we'da been treated better.

I question *America!* I used to say when I was working hard in the cotton fields, if I can just go to Washington—to the Justice Department—to the FBI—get close enough to let them know what was going on in Mississippi, I was sure that things would change in a week. Now that I have traveled across America, been to the Congress, to the Justice Department, to the FBI, I am faced with the things I'm not sure I wanted to find out. The sickness in Mississippi is not a Mississippi sickness. This is America's sickness.

What's gone help black people? What I really feel is necessary is that the black people in this country will have to upset this applecart. We can no longer ignore the fact that America is not the land of the free and the home of the brave . . . there is so much hypocrisy in America. The land of the free and the home of the brave is all on paper. It don't mean anything to us. The only way we can make this thing work is bring this thing out to the light that have been under the cover all these years. The scriptures have said, the things that have been done in the dark will be known on the housetops.

FANNIE LOU: (*from selected speeches*) Now that we have forced this man to give us welfare, our share of the taxes, where is we going to take it to? The question for black people is not when is the white man going to give us our rights, or when is he going to give us good education for our children, or when is he going to give us a job. If the white man gives you anything, just remember when he gets ready he will take it right back. We got to take it for ourselves.

I don't believe in separationism. A house divided against itself cannot stand, and neither can a nation. This country produces separatists. America is sick, and man is on the critical list.

They assassinated Dr. King, then passed a law telling us how good they is. In 1972, we can buy a home on their side of town, now how in hell can we do that when we can't pay the rent where we are now? But that law did have something in it for me: if I get three people there and tell 'em the truth, they'll put me in jail for conspiracy and inciting to riot. They didn't get Martin Luther King long as he was middle class, but when he said he would organize the poor folks, white and Indians as well as black, they said, "We gotta kill this nigger." And it ain't Memphis. It is the same kind of conspiracy killed King that killed Kennedy and killed Malcolm X. Now, they got the concentration camps ready and all I can say is we better be ready, we better be ready.

I'm never sure anymore when I leave home whether I'll get back or not. It seem like to tell the truth today is to run the risk of getting killed. But if I fall, I'll fall five feet four inches FORWARD in the fight for freedom. I'm not backing off of that, and nobody don't need to cover the ground I walk on as far as freedom is concerned!

Let's face it, what's hurting black folk that's without is hurting the white folk that's without! If the white folks fight for theyself, and the black folk fight for theyself, we gone crumble apart. These are things we gone have to fight together. We got to fight in America for all the people, and I'm perfectly willing to help make my country what it have to be.

Christianity is being concerned about your fellow man, not building a million-dollar church while people are starving right around the corner. Christ was a revolutionary person, out there in the streets where it was happening. That's what God is all about, and that's where I get my strength. We have to realize just how grave the problem is in the United States today and I think the sixth chapter of Ephesians, the eleventh and twelfth verses helps us to know . . . what it is we are up against. It says: "Put on the whole armor of God, that ye may be able to stand against the wiles of the devil. For we wrestle not against flesh and blood but against principalities, against powers, against the rulers of the darkness of this world, against spiritual wickedness in high places." This is what I think about when I think of my own work in the fight for freedom.

"And there was delivered unto him the book of the prophet Isaiah. And when he had opened the book he found the place where it is written, the spirit of the Lord is upon me, because he hath anointed me to preach the gospel to the poor; he hath sent me to heal the brokenhearted, to preach deliverance to the captives and recovering of sight to the blind, to set at liberty them that are bound, to preach the acceptable year of the Lord."

(*Sings*)

Precious Lord, take my hand,
Lead me on, let me stand.
I am tired, I am weak, I am worn.
Through the storm,
Through the night,
Lead me on to the light.
Take my hand precious Lord, lead me on.

THE END

ABOUT THE AUTHOR

BILLIE JEAN YOUNG lives in Pennington, Alabama, her hometown. She was educated in Choctaw County schools and holds degrees from Selma University, Judson College, and Samford University's Cumberland School of Law. A former Jackson State University Assistant Professor of Speech and Dramatic Art, she teaches at Mississippi State University Meridian campus. From the late 1960s into the early '90s, she was a national and international leader in development opportunities for rural women, especially African Americans. She co-founded and directed the Southern Rural Women's Network (SRWN) before writing and producing her best known work: *Fannie Lou Hamer: This Little Light...*, a one-woman play based on the life of the Mississippi Delta freedom fighter and human rights activist. In recognition of her work in preserving the history of African American women through the play and for her organizing work through the SRWN, Young was named a 1984 MacArthur Fellow by the John D. and Catherine T. MacArthur Foundation.